SINGAPORE

TRAVEL GUIDE 2024

Discover the history, traditions, cultural insight, must see Attractions, insider tips and best place to visit

JOHN S. MARLER

TABLE OF CONTENTS

INTRODUCTION

Welcome to the Lion City, where vibrant culture, rich history, and modern innovation come together to create an unforgettable travel experience. In this comprehensive Singapore travel guide for 2024, we invite you to discover the best that this dynamic city-state has to offer. Singapore, a bustling metropolis located at the crossroads of Asia, is a melting pot of countries, cuisines, and experiences. From its iconic skyline and world-class attractions to its bustling markets and vibrant neighbourhoods, Singapore offers something for every visitor. In this guide, you'll find everything you need to plan the perfect trip to Singapore. Whether you're interested in exploring the city's iconic landmarks, immersing yourself in its rich cultural history, or indulging in its delicious cuisine, we've got you covered. Discover the breathtaking beauty of Gardens by the Bay, marvel at the stunning views from Marina Bay Sands, and explore the vibrant areas of Chinatown, Little India, and Kampong Glam. Sample delicious street food at hawker centres, shop till you drop on Orchard Road, and experience the lively nightlife of Clarke Quay and Boat Quay. But Singapore is more than just a modern city—it's also a city of contrasts, where custom meets innovation at every turn. Explore the historic streets of Chinatown, visit ancient temples and mosques, and immerse yourself in the city's rich cultural history. Whether you're a first-time visitor or a seasoned tourist, Singapore never fails to captivate and inspire. So pack your bags, start on an unforgettable journey, and discover the magic of Singapore in 2024.

Get ready to discover the sights, sounds, and flavours of this incredible city-state. Your adventure starts here! Welcome to Singapore, where every moment is a new find and every experience is an unforgettable memory. Let the journey begin!

Overview of Singapore

Welcome to Singapore, a lively city-state located at the heart of Southeast Asia. Known for its stunning skyline, rich cultural tapestry, and world-class attractions, Singapore is a melting pot of countries, cuisines, and experiences. In this overview, we'll take you on a journey through the highlights of this dynamic city and help you plan an unforgettable trip to the Lion City.

A Modern Metropolis: Singapore is a bustling metropolis that seamlessly mixes custom and innovation. From its iconic skyline dotted with skyscrapers to its bustling streets filled with shops, restaurants, and attractions, Singapore is a city that never fails to amaze.

Rich Cultural Heritage: Despite its modernity, Singapore has managed to maintain its rich cultural heritage. The city is home to a diverse mix of cultures, including Chinese, Malay, Indian, and Eurasian, each of which has left its mark on the city's architecture, food, and customs.

Iconic Landmarks: Singapore is home to some of the most iconic buildings in the world. From the futuristic Marina Bay Sands to the historic Raffles Hotel, there's no lack of must-see attractions in the Lion City.

- **Marina Bay Sands:** This iconic hotel and entertainment complex is one of Singapore's most familiar landmarks. Featuring a stunning rooftop infinity pool, viewing deck, and world-class casino, Marina Bay Sands offers breathtaking views of the city skyline.

- Gardens by the Bay: Spanning 101 hectares, Gardens by the Bay is a beautiful horticultural oasis in the heart of Singapore. Explore the Flower Dome, Cloud Forest, and Supertree Grove, and wonder at the stunning displays of flowers, plants, and trees.

- Sentosa Island: Singapore's premier island resort spot, Sentosa Island is home to a wide range of attractions, including Universal Studios Singapore, S.E.A. Aquarium, and Adventure Cove Waterpark. Whether you're looking for thrills and excitement or rest and leisure, Sentosa Island has something for everyone.

World-Class Dining: Singapore is a paradise for food lovers, with a diverse range of culinary delights to fit every palate and budget. From hawker centres and street food carts to Michelin-starred restaurants and fine dining establishments, Singapore offers a culinary experience like no other.

Shopping Paradise: Singapore is also a shopper's paradise, with an abundance of malls, boutiques, and markets to discover. Whether you're looking for name brands, unique souvenirs, or bargain buys, you'll find it all in Singapore.

Efficient Public Transportation: Getting around Singapore is easy and quick, thanks to its efficient public transportation system. The city is covered by an extensive network of buses, trains, and taxis, making it easy to explore all that Singapore has to offer.

Warm Hospitality: Last but not least, Singapore is known for its warm welcome and friendly locals. Whether you're dining at a hawker centre, shopping in a local market, or visiting the city's attractions, you'll always be greeted with a smile and a warm welcome.

Brief History

Singapore's history is as rich and diverse as its culture, with a story that spans centuries and includes a tapestry of cultures, traditions, and influences. In this part, we'll take you on a journey through the key events and milestones that have shaped Singapore into the dynamic city-state it is today.

Early Settlements: The oldest records of Singapore date back to the 14th century, when the island was known as

Temasek, or "Sea Town" in Javanese. The island was a thriving trade post, attracting merchants from China, India, and the Malay Archipelago.

Colonial Era: In the early 19th century, Singapore came under British rule after Sir Stamford Raffles built a trading post on the island in 1819. Under British colonial rule, Singapore thrived as a centre of trade and commerce, attracting immigrants from China, India, and other parts of Asia.

World War II: During World War II, Singapore was controlled by the Japanese from 1942 to 1945. The Japanese occupation was a dark time in Singapore's history, marked by widespread suffering and hardship.

Independence: Singapore got independence from Britain in 1963 and became a part of Malaysia. However, racial and political tensions led to Singapore's separation from Malaysia in 1965, and the island claimed independence as the Republic of Singapore.

Rapid Development: In the years following independence, Singapore experienced rapid growth and modernization under the leadership of its first Prime Minister, Lee Kuan Yew. The government implemented a number of economic policies aimed at transforming Singapore into a global financial and business hub.

Multicultural Society: Today, Singapore is a vibrant multicultural society, with a population that shows its diverse ethnic and cultural heritage. The city-state is home to Chinese, Malay, Indian, and Eurasian communities, each of which has added to Singapore's unique identity.

Key Historical Sites:

- **Raffles Hotel:** Built in 1887, Raffles Hotel is one of Singapore's most iconic landmarks and a symbol of the city's colonial history. The hotel has played home to many famous guests over the years, including writers, politicians, and celebrities.

- **Chinatown:** Explore the historic streets of Chinatown and learn its rich cultural heritage. Visit the Buddha Tooth Relic Temple, explore the bustling streets filled with shops and markets, and taste delicious street food at the hawker centres.

- **Little India:** Immerse yourself in the sights, sounds, and smells of Little India, Singapore's lively Indian neighbourhood. Visit the Sri Veeramakaliamman Temple, explore the colourful shops and markets, and taste authentic Indian cuisine.

Singapore's past is a fascinating tale of resilience, adaptation, and transformation. From its humble beginnings as a trading post to its rise as a global economic powerhouse, Singapore has faced many challenges to become the dynamic city-state it is today. By exploring the city's key historical sites and landmarks, visitors can gain a better understanding of Singapore's rich cultural heritage and the forces that have shaped its identity. So, pack your bags, step back in time, and discover the fascinating past of Singapore firsthand!

Chapter 1

Travel Planning

Welcome to the part of your ultimate Singapore guide where you can plan your trip! Making plans for your trip to this lively island nation is the first thing that will help you have an experience you will never forget. This part has all the important information you need to have a great time in Singapore, whether it's your first time there or you're coming back to see more.

Best Time to Go:
Singapore has a warm, tropical climate that makes it a great place to visit any time of the year. But the best time to go relies on what you want to do. People usually agree that the best times to visit are from February to April and from July to August, when the weather is cool and pleasant.

Requirements for a visa:

Make sure you know what kind of visa you need for Singapore before you pack your bags. Many travellers can enter Singapore without a visa, but it's important to ensure you have the necessary documentation. Most visitors are given either a 30 or 90 day stay upon arrival, but it's always wise to double check the latest regulations before your trip.

Budgeting Tips:

Singapore offers a wide range of experiences to fit every budget. Whether you're a luxury tourist or backpacking on a shoestring, there's something for everyone. To make the most of your budget, consider buying a Singapore Tourist Pass for unlimited travel on public transportation. Additionally, take advantage of the city's hawker centres, where you can taste delicious local cuisine at affordable prices.

Accommodation:

Choosing the right accommodation is crucial for a comfy and enjoyable stay. Singapore boasts a diverse range of choices, from budget friendly hotels to luxurious five star hotels. If you're looking to immerse yourself in the city's vibrant culture, try staying in the bustling areas of Chinatown or Little India. Alternatively, if you prefer a more tranquil experience, Sentosa Island offers luxurious resorts with gorgeous ocean views.

Getting to Singapore:

Singapore is easily approachable from around the world, thanks to its world class airport and efficient public transportation system. Changi Airport, consistently ranked as one of the best airports worldwide, serves as a major hub for international flights. Once you arrive, getting to the city centre is quick and convenient, with various transportation choices available, including the MRT, taxis, and airport shuttles.

Transportation:

Getting around Singapore is a breeze, thanks to its fast and well connected public transportation system. The Mass Rapid Transit (MRT) network offers a convenient way to explore the city, with trains running regularly to all major sites and neighbourhoods. For those who prefer more flexibility, taxis and ridesharing services are easily available. Alternatively, you can explore the city on foot. or rent a bicycle for a more relaxed experience.

Travel Planning Tips: Book your accommodation in advance, especially during peak tourist seasons.
Download useful travel apps, such as transport maps and translation tools, to make navigating Singapore easy.
Familiarise yourself with Singapore's local customs and etiquette to ensure a smooth and respectful journey experience.

With careful planning and preparation, your Singapore adventure is sure to be an amazing experience. So pack your bags, prepare your itinerary, and get ready to discover all that this dynamic citystate has to offer!

Best Time to Visit

Choosing the perfect time to visit Singapore can significantly improve your experience of this vibrant island city-state. With its tropical climate and year-round warm temperatures, Singapore welcomes tourists at any time of the year. However, to make the most of your trip and enjoy all that Singapore has to offer, it's important to consider the weather, festivals, and events happening throughout the year.

Weather Overview:
Singapore gets a consistent tropical climate, characterised by hot and humid weather year-round. The temperature usually ranges between 25°C to 31°C (77°F to 88°F), making it the perfect destination for sun-seekers and beach lovers. However, the island does experience two different monsoon seasons, which can influence your travel plans.

Dry Season (February to April):
The months between February and April are considered some of the best times to visit Singapore. During this time, the island experiences drier weather with minimal rainfall and lower humidity levels. The skies are often

clear, making it great for outdoor activities and exploring Singapore's numerous attractions.

Peak Tourist Season (July to August):
Another popular time to visit Singapore is during the months of July and August. While the weather can be slightly hotter and more humid during this time, it overlaps with the school holidays in many countries, making it an ideal time for families to visit. Additionally, Singapore's National Day comes on August 9th, bringing with it a host of festivities, including fireworks, parades, and cultural performances.

Festivals and Events:
One of the best ways to experience Singapore's vibrant culture is by visiting one of its many festivals and events. From traditional celebrations to world-class performances, there's always something exciting going on the island. Some of the must-see events include:

- Chinese New Year (January/February): Experience the vibrant festivities, including lion dances, street performances, and the famous Chingay Parade.

- Singapore International Festival of Arts (May to June): Immerse yourself in a diverse range of arts and cultural events from around the world.

- Singapore Food Festival (July): Indulge in Singapore's diverse culinary scene with mouthwatering food tastings, cooking workshops, and food-themed events.

- Deepavali (October/November): Join in the celebrations of the Hindu holiday of lights with colourful decorations, cultural performances, and delicious Indian cuisine.

Off-Peak Season (November to January):

While Singapore is a popular year-round location, the months between November and January are considered the off-peak season for tourism. During this time, the island gets slightly higher rainfall and humidity levels. However, this also means fewer crowds, making it an excellent time to explore Singapore's sites at your own pace.

Visa Requirements

Before embarking on your journey to Singapore, it's important to understand the visa requirements to ensure a smooth and hassle-free travel experience. Fortunately, for many travellers, entering Singapore is a straightforward process, with lenient visa rules allowing visitors from different countries to enter without a visa. Here's what you need to know:

Visa-Free Entry:
Citizens of many countries are eligible for visa-free entry into Singapore for short stays. These countries include the United States, Canada, the United Kingdom, Australia, New Zealand, and most European states. Under the visa-free entry scheme, travellers are usually granted either a 30 or 90-day stay upon arrival, based on their nationality.

Tourist Visa Extension:
If you wish to extend your stay in Singapore beyond the allowed visa-free period, you can apply for a tourist visa

extension. The extension allows you to stay for an additional 30 days, giving you more time to explore everything that Singapore has to offer. To apply for a visa extension, you can visit the Immigration & Checkpoints Authority (ICA) online or apply in person at the ICA Building.

Electronic Arrival Card:

For travellers from select countries, Singapore has adopted an electronic arrival card system, making the entry process even more convenient. Instead of filling out a paper arrival card, eligible travellers can send their arrival information online before their trip. The electronic arrival card is valid for visits of up to 90 days for tourism or business reasons.

Special Passes:

In certain cases, visitors may require a special pass to enter Singapore. This includes travellers who are coming for medical treatment, attending conferences or exhibitions, or engaging in sporting events. If you're unsure whether you need a special pass, it's best to check with the closest Singaporean embassy or consulate before your trip.

Additional Entry Requirements:

While Singapore has relatively lenient visa requirements, there are a few extra entry requirements that travellers should be aware of:

- Your passport must be valid for at least six months beyond your planned stay.
- You must have proof of sufficient funds to cover your stay in Singapore.
- You may be asked to show proof of onward or return travel.

Visa Application Process:

For travellers who require a visa to enter Singapore, the application process is straightforward and can usually be finished online. The process typically includes filling out an online application form, providing supporting documents, and paying the visa fee. Once approved, you will receive an electronic visa (e-visa) that you can print and show upon arrival in Singapore.

Budgeting Tips

Exploring Singapore doesn't have to break the bank! With a little planning and some insider tips, you can enjoy all that this lively island city-state has to offer without blowing your budget. From affordable accommodations to budget-friendly dining choices, here are some budgeting tips to help you make the most of your Singapore adventure:

1. Plan Your Budget: Before you set off on your Singapore adventure, take some time to plan your spending. Consider how much you want to spend on accommodation, dining, transportation, and events. Having a budget in mind will help you make smart spending choices and ensure you don't overspend during your trip.

2. Choose Affordable Accommodation: Singapore offers a wide range of accommodation options to fit every budget. If you're looking to save money, try staying in budget-friendly hostels or guesthouses. These choices often provide clean and comfortable accommodations at

a fraction of the cost of hotels. Alternatively, you can look for budget-friendly hotels or Airbnb choices in less touristy areas of the city.

3. Take Advantage of Public Transportation: Getting around Singapore is easy and cheap thanks to its efficient public transportation system. The Mass Rapid Transit (MRT) network provides easy access to all major attractions and neighbourhoods. Consider buying a Singapore Tourist Pass, which offers unlimited travel on public transportation for a fixed fee. This can save you money compared to getting individual tickets for each journey.

4. Eat Like a Local: One of the best things about Singapore is its amazing food scene, and you don't have to spend a fortune to eat well. Head to one of the city's many hawker centres or food courts to taste delicious and affordable local cuisine. From flavorful laksa and chicken rice to mouthwatering satay and roti prata, there's something for every taste and budget.

5. Look for Free and Low-Cost Activities: There are plenty of free and low-cost things to enjoy in Singapore. Take a leisurely walk through the beautiful Gardens by

the Bay, explore the colourful neighbourhoods of Chinatown and Little India, or visit one of the city's many museums and art galleries during their free admission days. Additionally, many parks and nature reserves offer free entry, allowing you to enjoy Singapore's natural beauty without paying a dime.

6. Shop Smart: Singapore is known for its shopping, but that doesn't mean you have to break the bank. Look for budget-friendly shopping choices such as street markets, flea markets, and outlet malls, where you can find great deals on clothing, electronics, and souvenirs. Additionally, keep an eye out for sales and deals at shopping malls and department stores, where you can score big discounts on designer brands and luxury goods.

7. Stay Hydrated and Save on Drinks: Singapore's tropical climate means it's important to stay hydrated, especially when you're out exploring. Instead of buying bottled water, carry a refillable water bottle and fill up at one of the city's many water stations or public taps. Additionally, if you're planning to enjoy a few drinks, look for happy hour deals and drink promotions at bars and restaurants to save money on your night out.

8. Take Advantage of Free Wi-Fi: Many public places in Singapore offer free Wi-Fi, including MRT stations, shopping malls, and hawker centres. Take advantage of these free Wi-Fi places to stay connected without racking up expensive roaming charges.

By following these planning tips, you can enjoy all that Singapore has to offer without breaking the bank. With a little planning and some smart spending decisions, you can make the most of your Singapore trip and create memories that will last a lifetime. So pack your bags, prepare your budget, and get ready for an amazing trip to the Lion City!

Chapter 2

Getting to Singapore

Singapore, with its modern infrastructure and world-class transportation systems, is easily approachable from all corners of the globe. Whether you're coming by air, land, or sea, getting to Singapore is simple and convenient. Here's everything you need to know about going to this vibrant island city-state:

From the air:

Changi Airport, consistently ranked as one of the best airports in the world, serves as Singapore's main gateway for foreign travellers. Located on the eastern edge of the island, Changi Airport is well-connected to major places around the world, with over 100 airlines operating flights to and from Singapore.

Direct Flights:

Many major airlines offer direct flights to Singapore from key places worldwide, making it easy to reach the island without the need for layovers or connecting flights. Some of the companies offering direct flights to Singapore include Singapore companies, Emirates, Qantas, British Airways, and United Airlines.

Connecting Flights:

If there are no direct flights available from your departure city, you can easily reach Singapore via connecting flights through big hub airports such as Dubai, Hong Kong, Tokyo, and Kuala Lumpur. With numerous daily flights connecting Singapore to cities around the world, you'll have no trouble finding a convenient route to your location.

Airport Facilities:

Upon arrival at Changi Airport, you'll find a wide range of services to make your travel experience as comfortable as possible. From duty-free shopping and eating options to relaxation lounges and entertainment areas, Changi Airport has everything you need to relax and unwind after your flight.

From the Land:

While most visitors arrive in Singapore by air, it's also possible to join the island by land from neighbouring Malaysia. Singapore is linked to the Malaysian mainland by a causeway and a bridge, making it easy to reach by bus, car, or train.

Bus:

Several bus companies run regular services between Singapore and various cities in Malaysia, including Kuala Lumpur, Malacca, and Johor Bahru. The trip from Kuala Lumpur to Singapore by bus takes approximately five to six hours, depending on traffic conditions.

Train:

For a more scenic trip, you can travel to Singapore from Malaysia by train. The KTM Intercity train runs services between Singapore and Kuala Lumpur, as well as other cities in Malaysia. The train journey offers stunning views of the Malaysian countryside and is a popular choice for travellers looking to explore the region at a leisurely pace.

By Sea:

If you're arriving in Singapore from nearby islands or other countries in the area, you can also travel by sea. Singapore is one of the busiest seaports in the world, with numerous cruise ships and ferries coming and departing from its shores each day.

Cruise Ships:

Many cruise lines include Singapore as a port of call on their Southeast Asia routes. Singapore's cruise terminal, located at Marina Bay Cruise Centre, is equipped to handle large cruise ships and offers a wide range of facilities for passengers, including duty-free shopping, dining choices, and transportation services.

Ferries:

Several ferry companies run services between Singapore and nearby Indonesian islands such as Batam and Bintan. The ferry journey takes approximately 45 minutes to two hours, based on your destination, and offers a convenient and cost-effective way to explore the region.

Air Travel

Flying to Singapore is the fastest and most convenient way to start your trip in this vibrant island city-state. Singapore is well-connected to important cities around the world, with Changi Airport serving as one of the busiest and most efficient airports globally. Here's everything you need to know to make your air travel experience to Singapore as easy and enjoyable as possible:

Changi Airport - Your Gateway to Singapore:
Welcome to Changi Airport, regularly ranked as one of the best airports in the world. Located on the eastern edge of Singapore, Changi Airport serves as the main gateway for foreign travellers. With its modern facilities, efficient services, and world-class amenities, Changi Airport ensures that your trip to Singapore starts off on

the right foot.

Direct Flights:

Many major airlines offer direct flights to Singapore from key places worldwide, making it easy to reach the island without the need for layovers or connecting flights. Whether you're flying from New York, London, Sydney, or Tokyo, you'll find a range of direct flight choices to suit your schedule and budget. Singapore Airlines, the national carrier of Singapore, offers direct flights from major places worldwide and is renowned for its exceptional service and comfortable travel experience.

Connecting Flights:

If there are no direct flights available from your departure place, don't worry! Singapore is well-connected to major hub airports around the world, making it easy to reach with connecting flights. With numerous daily flights connecting Singapore to cities across Asia, Europe, North America, and beyond, you'll have no trouble finding a convenient route to your location. Major airlines such as Emirates, Qatar Airways, Cathay Pacific, and Korean Air run connecting flights to Singapore, offering seamless travel experiences with convenient layover times and excellent onboard services.

Airport Facilities:
Upon arrival at Changi Airport, you'll be greeted by a wide range of facilities to make your flight experience as comfortable and enjoyable as possible. Changi Airport boasts three main terminals, each offering a variety of services, including duty-free shopping, dining choices, relaxation lounges, entertainment areas, and transit hotels. Whether you're looking to indulge in some shopping therapy, enjoy a delicious meal, or simply relax and unwind before your next flight, Changi Airport has everything you need to make the most of your layover.

Transit Passengers:
If you have a layover in Singapore, Changi Airport offers complimentary tours and attractions for transit passengers, allowing you to explore the city's top sites without leaving the airport. From free city tours to movie

theatres, rooftop swimming pools, and butterfly gardens, there's plenty to see and do at Changi Airport to keep you busy during your layover.

Flying to Singapore is the fastest, most convenient, and comfortable way to start your trip in this vibrant island city-state. With its modern infrastructure, efficient services, and world-class amenities, Changi Airport ensures that your trip to Singapore is as smooth and enjoyable as possible. So sit back, relax, and get ready to start on an unforgettable adventure in the Lion City!

Land and Sea Entry Points

While flying is the most popular way to reach Singapore, there are also options for travellers who prefer to arrive by land or sea. Whether you're crossing the Causeway from Malaysia or coming by cruise ship, getting to Singapore by land or sea offers a unique and memorable travel experience. Here's everything you need to know about land and sea entry points to Singapore:

Crossing the Causeway: Johor-Singapore Causeway: The Johor-Singapore bridge is a 1,056-metre-long bridge that connects Singapore to the southern tip of the Malaysian peninsula. This iconic bridge spans the Straits of Johor and serves as one of the key entry points for travellers coming to Singapore by land. Whether you're going by bus, car, or train, crossing the Causeway is a convenient and efficient way to reach Singapore from Malaysia.

Bus Services: Several bus companies run regular services between Singapore and various cities in Malaysia, including Kuala Lumpur, Malacca, and Johor Bahru. The trip from Kuala Lumpur to Singapore by bus takes approximately five to six hours, depending on traffic conditions, making it a convenient and affordable choice for budget-conscious travellers.

Train Services: For a more scenic trip, you can travel to Singapore from Malaysia by train. The KTM Intercity train runs services between Singapore and Kuala Lumpur, as well as other cities in Malaysia. The train journey offers stunning views of the Malaysian countryside and is a popular choice for travellers looking to explore the region at a leisurely pace.

Second Link Bridge: In addition to the Johor-Singapore Causeway, Singapore is also linked to Malaysia by the Second Link Bridge. This bridge, officially known as the Malaysia-Singapore Second Link, spans the Straits of Johor and offers an alternative route for travellers arriving from Malaysia. The Second Link Bridge is less congested than the Causeway, making it a popular choice for travellers looking to escape traffic jams and long queues.

Arriving by Sea: Cruise Ships: Many cruise lines include Singapore as a port of call on their Southeast Asia itineraries, making it easy to work a visit to Singapore into your cruise vacation. Singapore's cruise terminal, located at Marina Bay Cruise Centre, is equipped to handle large cruise ships and offers a wide range of facilities for passengers, including duty-free shopping, dining choices, and transportation services.

Ferries: Several ferry companies run services between Singapore and nearby Indonesian islands such as Batam and Bintan. The ferry journey takes approximately 45 minutes to two hours, based on your destination, and offers a convenient and cost-effective way to explore the region. With frequent departures throughout the day, you'll have no trouble finding a ferry that fits your plan.

Chapter 3

Transportation

Getting around Singapore is easy and handy, thanks to its efficient and well-connected transportation system. Whether you prefer to travel by train, bus, taxi, or ride-sharing service, Singapore offers a variety of transportation choices to suit every traveller's needs. Here's everything you need to know about getting around Singapore:

Mass Rapid Transit (MRT):

The Backbone of Singapore's Transportation System:

The Mass Rapid Transit (MRT) system is the backbone of Singapore's transportation network, offering fast, efficient, and cheap travel around the island. With an extensive network of lines and stops covering almost every part of Singapore, the MRT is the preferred mode of transportation for both locals and tourists alike.

Convenient and Reliable:

The MRT system works from early morning until late at night, with trains running at regular intervals. With air-conditioned trains and stops, comfortable seating, and clear signage in multiple languages, navigating the MRT system is easy and hassle-free.

Singapore Tourist Pass:

For travellers looking for unlimited travel on Singapore's public transportation system, the Singapore Tourist Pass is the perfect choice. Available for one, two, or three days, the tourist pass offers unlimited rides on buses, MRT trains, and LRT trains for a set fee. With the tourist pass, you can explore Singapore's top attractions without having to worry about buying individual tickets for each journey.

Bus Services:

Comprehensive Bus Network:

In addition to the MRT system, Singapore also boasts an extensive network of bus routes that cover even the most remote parts of the island. With over 300 bus services running around the clock, getting around Singapore by bus is convenient and affordable.

Comfortable and Air-Conditioned:
Singapore's buses are modern, comfortable, and air-conditioned, making them a pleasant way to move around the island. With designated seating for elderly and disabled passengers, as well as priority queues at bus stops, Singapore's bus system is meant to be available to all travellers.

EZ-Link Card:
For frequent bus travellers, the EZ-Link card is a convenient way to pay for your travels. Similar to a prepaid debit card, the EZ-Link card lets you top up credit and use it to pay for bus and MRT rides. Simply tap your card on the card reader when boarding and alighting the bus, and the fare will be immediately deducted from your balance.

Taxi and Ride-Sharing Services:
Convenient and Comfortable:

For travellers looking for a more comfortable and convenient way to get around Singapore, taxis and ride-sharing services are easily available. With thousands of taxis running on the island, you'll have no trouble finding a ride, even during peak hours.

Grab and Gojek:
In addition to traditional taxis, ride-sharing services such as Grab and Gojek also run in Singapore, offering an alternative to traditional taxi services. With the ease of booking a ride through a mobile app and the option to pay by credit card, ride-sharing services are becoming an increasingly popular choice for travellers.

Public Transportation

Singapore boasts one of the most efficient and well-connected public transportation systems in the world, making it easy for guests to explore the city's many attractions. Here's everything you need to know about getting around Singapore using public transportation:

Mass Rapid Transit (MRT):

The Mass Rapid Transit (MRT) system is the backbone of Singapore's public transportation network, giving fast and convenient travel around the island. With an extensive network of lines and stations, the MRT makes it easy to reach almost any place in Singapore. Each MRT station is equipped with clear signage, ticket machines, and route maps to help you manage the system. Trains run from early morning until late at night, with gaps of just a few minutes between each train during peak hours.

For visitors looking for unlimited travel on Singapore's public transportation system, the Singapore Tourist Pass is an excellent choice. Available for one, two, or three days, the tourist pass offers unlimited rides on buses, MRT trains, and LRT trains for a set fee.

Bus Services:

Singapore also boasts an extensive network of bus routes that cover every corner of the island. With over 300 bus services running around the clock, getting around

Singapore by bus is convenient and affordable. Each bus is provided with air conditioning, comfortable seating, and priority queues at bus stops. Many buses also have designated seating for elderly and disabled passengers, making them available to all travellers.

For frequent bus travellers, the EZ-Link card is a convenient way to pay for your travels. Similar to a prepaid debit card, the EZ-Link card lets you top up credit and use it to pay for bus and MRT rides. Simply tap your card on the card reader when boarding and alighting the bus, and the fare will be immediately deducted from your balance.

Taxi and Ride-Sharing Services:

For travellers looking for a more comfortable and convenient way to get around Singapore, taxis and ride-sharing services are easily available. With thousands of taxis running on the island, you'll have no trouble finding a ride, even during peak hours.

In addition to traditional taxis, ride-sharing services such as Grab and Gojek also run in Singapore, offering an alternative to traditional taxi services. With the ease of booking a ride through a mobile app and the option to pay by credit card, ride-sharing services are becoming an increasingly popular choice for travellers.

With its efficient and well-connected public transportation system, getting around Singapore is easy and handy. Whether you prefer to travel by MRT, bus, taxi, or ride-sharing service, Singapore offers a variety of transportation options to meet every traveller's needs. So leave the car behind and discover all that this vibrant island city-state has to offer using public transportation!

Rental Cars, Taxis, and Ridesharing Services

While Singapore's public transportation system is efficient and well-connected, there are times when visitors may prefer the convenience of renting a car, taking a taxi, or using a ridesharing service to get around the city. Here's everything you need to know about these transportation options:

Rental Cars:

Renting a car in Singapore is a convenient option for tourists who want the freedom to explore the city at their own pace. While Singapore is relatively small and easy to navigate, having a rental car allows you to visit sites that may be off the beaten path and explore the island at your leisure.

There are several car rental companies operating in Singapore, offering a wide range of vehicles to suit every budget and taste. Whether you're looking for a compact car for city driving or a large SUV for exploring the countryside, you'll find plenty of options to choose from.

Before renting a car in Singapore, it's important to familiarise yourself with the local traffic rules and regulations. Singapore has strict traffic laws, including speed limits, seatbelt requirements, and drink-driving laws, so be sure to drive safely and properly during your stay.

Taxis:

Taxis are a convenient and efficient way to get around Singapore, especially if you're travelling to places that may not be easily accessible by public transportation. With thousands of taxis running on the island, you'll have no trouble finding a ride, even during peak hours.

Singapore's taxis are provided with air conditioning, comfortable seating, and metres to figure the fare. Taxis can be hailed on the street, booked in advance, or found at taxi stands spread throughout the city. Simply tell the driver your location, and they'll take you there safely and efficiently.

While taxis in Singapore are usually safe and reliable, it's essential to be aware of potential scams or overcharging. Always ensure that the taxi metre is turned on at the beginning of your trip and ask for a receipt at the end. If you have any worries about the fare, don't hesitate to ask the driver for clarification.

Ridesharing Services:

In addition to traditional taxis, ridesharing services such as Grab and Gojek also run in Singapore, offering an alternative to traditional taxi services. With the ease of booking a ride through a mobile app and the option to pay by credit card, ridesharing services are becoming an increasingly popular choice for travellers. Ridesharing services offer a range of vehicle choices, including standard cars, premium vehicles, and larger vehicles for groups or families. Whether you're travelling alone or with a group, you'll find a ridesharing option to fit your needs and budget.

In addition to providing transportation around the city, ridesharing services also offer other services such as food delivery and package delivery, making them a convenient option for travellers looking for a one-stop answer for their transportation needs.

Chapter 4

Accommodation

Finding Your Home Away from Home in Singapore Finding the right accommodation is an important part of any travel experience, and in Singapore, you'll find a wide range of options to suit every budget and preference. From luxury hotels to budget-friendly hostels, cosy guesthouses, and stylish boutique hotels, Singapore offers something for every type of tourist. Here's everything you need to know about finding the right place to stay in Singapore:

Luxury Hotels:

If you're looking for a luxurious and indulgent experience, Singapore boasts some of the best hotels in the world. From iconic landmarks like the Marina Bay Sands to award-winning hotels like The Ritz-Carlton and The Fullerton Hotel, you'll find no lack of luxury accommodation options in Singapore. Luxury hotels in Singapore offer world-class amenities, including luxury rooms and suites, stunning rooftop pools, Michelin-starred restaurants, and luxurious spa facilities. Whether you're looking for a romantic getaway, a family vacation, or a business trip, you'll find the right luxury hotel to suit your needs in Singapore.

Boutique Hotels:

For visitors looking for a more intimate and unique experience, boutique hotels are an excellent choice. Singapore is home to a lively boutique hotel scene, with stylish and chic properties located in some of the city's trendiest neighbourhoods. Boutique hotels in Singapore offer personalised service, stylish decor, and a range of unique features, including rooftop bars, art galleries, and cosy lounges. Whether you're looking for a trendy boutique hotel in the heart of the city or a cosy boutique hotel in a quiet area, you'll find plenty of options to choose from in Singapore.

Budget-Friendly Accommodation:

Travelling on a budget? Not to worry! Singapore offers plenty of budget-friendly accommodation options to meet every traveller's needs. From affordable hostels and guesthouses to budget-friendly hotels and Airbnb homes, you'll find plenty of options to choose from without breaking the bank. Hostels and guesthouses in Singapore offer clean and comfortable accommodations at a fraction of the cost of standard hotels. Many hostels also offer amenities such as free breakfast, shared kitchens, and social activities, making them a popular choice for budget-conscious travellers looking to meet fellow travellers and make new friends.

Serviced Apartments:

For travellers looking for a home away from home, serviced apartments are an excellent choice. Singapore offers a wide range of serviced apartments, running from studio apartments to spacious penthouses, all equipped with modern amenities and facilities.

Serviced apartments in Singapore offer the convenience of a hotel with the comfort of home, with amenities such as fully equipped kitchens, separate living and eating areas, and in-room laundry facilities. Whether you're travelling for business or pleasure, a serviced apartment offers the perfect base for your stay in Singapore.

No matter what your budget or taste, finding the perfect accommodation in Singapore is easy. From luxury hotels to budget-friendly hostels, cosy guesthouses, and stylish boutique hotels, Singapore offers something for every type of tourist. So whether you're looking for a luxurious retreat, a trendy boutique hotel, or a budget-friendly hostel, you'll find the right place to stay in Singapore.

Overview of Neighbourhoods

Singapore is a melting pot of cultures, and each of its neighbourhoods offers a unique and distinct experience for visitors. From the bustling streets of Chinatown to the trendy cafes of Tiong Bahru, the vibrant nightlife of Clarke Quay, and the lush greenery of Sentosa Island, Singapore's areas have something for everyone. Here's an overview of some of the most famous neighbourhoods in Singapore:

Marina Bay:

Marina Bay is Singapore's modern and glamorous district, home to some of the city's most iconic landmarks and sights. Here, you'll find the stunning Marina Bay Sands hotel and casino, the futuristic Gardens by the Bay, and the famous Merlion statue. In addition to its famous landmarks, Marina Bay also offers a wealth of shopping, dining, and entertainment choices. The Marina Bay Sands complex is home to a luxury shopping mall, world-class restaurants, and a vibrant nightlife scene, making it the perfect spot for travellers looking for a taste of Singapore's glitz and glamour.

Chinatown:

Step back in time and explore Singapore's rich Chinese history in Chinatown. Here, you'll find bright heritage shophouses, bustling street markets, and an array of traditional Chinese temples and shrines.

Chinatown is also a food lover's paradise, with countless hawker stalls, traditional eateries, and trendy restaurants serving up real Chinese cuisine. Don't miss the chance to try classic dishes like chicken rice, char , and chilli crab during your visit to Chinatown.

Little India:

Experience the sights, sounds, and smells of India in Singapore's lively Little India neighbourhood. Here, you'll find bustling streets lined with bright shops, aromatic spice stalls, and traditional Indian eateries. Little India is also home to several historic sites, including the Sri Veeramakaliamman Temple and the bustling Mustafa Centre, a 24-hour shopping mall that sells everything from electronics to textiles to groceries.

Tiong Bahru:

Tiong Bahru is one of Singapore's trendiest areas, known for its charming art deco architecture, trendy cafes, and boutique shops. Take a leisurely stroll through the neighbourhood's leafy streets and find hidden gems around every corner.

Tiong Bahru is also home to some of Singapore's best food, with a wide range of eateries serving up everything from traditional Singaporean fare to modern fusion dishes. Don't miss the chance to visit the Tiong Bahru Market, where you'll find a busy hawker centre serving up some of the city's best local fare.

Sentosa Island: Escape the hustle and bustle of the city and relax on the clean beaches of Sentosa Island. This idyllic island paradise is home to some of Singapore's best sites, including Universal Studios Singapore, S.E.A. Aquarium, and Adventure Cove Waterpark.
In addition to its attractions, Sentosa Island also offers a range of dining, shopping, and entertainment choices, making it the perfect destination for a day of fun in the sun.

With its diverse neighbourhoods, Singapore gives something for every type of traveller. Whether you're looking to explore the city's rich cultural heritage, indulge in world-class shopping and dining, or simply relax on the beach, you'll find the right neighbourhood to suit your interests and preferences. So pack your bags and get ready to explore all that Singapore has to offer!

Recommended Hotels, Hostels, and Guesthouses

Finding the right place to stay in Singapore can make all the difference in your travel experience. Whether you're looking for luxury, budget-friendly accommodation, or something in between, Singapore has a wide range of choices to suit every traveller's needs. Here are some suggested hotels, hostels, and guesthouses to consider for your stay in Singapore:

Luxury Hotels:

1. Marina Bay Sands: - Experience luxury at its best at Marina Bay Sands, Singapore's most iconic hotel. - Enjoy stunning views of the city skyline from the hotel's infinity pool, the world's biggest rooftop pool. - Indulge in world-class dining at one of the hotel's famous chef restaurants, including CUT by Wolfgang Puck and LAVO Italian Restaurant & Rooftop Bar.

2. The Ritz-Carlton, Millenia Singapore: - Treat yourself to a luxury stay at The Ritz-Carlton, Millenia Singapore.

- Relax and unwind in large and elegant rooms and suites with stunning views of Marina Bay.
- Indulge in fine dining experiences at the hotel's award-winning restaurants, including Summer Pavilion and Colony.

Boutique Hotels:

1. Lloyd's Inn: - Experience tranquillity in the heart of the city at Lloyd's Inn, a stylish boutique hotel set in Singapore's Orchard Road neighbourhood. - Relax in simple yet stylish rooms and suites with sleek modern design and thoughtful amenities. - Enjoy the hotel's tranquil garden and rooftop terrace, great for relaxation and unwinding after a day of exploring the city.

2. Hotel Mono: - Immerse yourself in Singapore's rich history at Hotel Mono, a stylish boutique hotel located in the historic Chinatown district. - Stay in beautifully designed rooms featuring sleek monochrome interiors and modern amenities. - Explore the vibrant neighbourhood of Chinatown with its bustling street markets, traditional eateries, and historic sites.

Budget-Friendly Accommodation:

1. The Pod @ Beach Road Boutique Capsule Hotel:

- Experience affordable luxury at The Pod @ Beach Road, a stylish boutique capsule hotel located in the heart of Singapore's historic Kampong Glam neighbourhood. - Stay in sleek and modern capsules supplied with personal TVs, power sockets, and reading lights. - Enjoy the hotel's rooftop garden and lounge area, great for relaxing and socialising with fellow travellers.

2. Dream Lodge: - Enjoy a comfortable and affordable stay at Dream Lodge, a cosy guesthouse located in the lively Little India neighbourhood.

- Stay in clean and cosy dormitory-style rooms or private rooms with modern amenities.

- Explore the colourful streets of Little India with its bustling markets, aromatic food stalls, and lively cultural landmarks.

Hostels:

1. The Bohemian Chic Hostel: - Experience bohemian

charm at The Bohemian Chic Hostel, a cosy and friendly hostel located in the trendy Tiong Bahru neighbourhood.

- Stay in stylish and comfy dormitory-style rooms with modern amenities and thoughtful touches.
- Explore the hip area of Tiong Bahru with its trendy cafes, boutique shops, and art galleries.

2. Bunc Hostel: - Experience budget-friendly luxury at Bunc Hostel, a stylish and modern hostel located in Singapore's bustling Bugis area.

- Stay in sleek and comfortable dormitory-style rooms or private rooms with modern amenities and stylish decor. - Enjoy the hotel's lively communal spaces, including a rooftop terrace, movie lounge, and social kitchen.

Budget to Luxury Accommodations

Finding the right accommodation in Singapore can make or break your travel experience. Whether you're on a tight budget or looking to splurge on luxury, Singapore offers a wide range of accommodation choices to suit every traveller's needs. From budget-friendly hostels and guesthouses to luxurious hotels and resorts, here are some suggested places to stay in Singapore:

Budget Accommodations:

1. Dream Lodge: - Located in the vibrant Little India neighbourhood, Dream Lodge offers affordable accommodation without compromising on luxury.

- Choose from dormitory-style rooms or private rooms, all equipped with modern amenities and cosy furnishings.

- Enjoy the hostel's communal spaces, including a rooftop terrace and lounge area, great for socialising and meeting fellow travellers.

2. The Pod @ Beach Road Boutique Capsule Hotel:

- Experience affordable luxury at The Pod @ Beach Road, a stylish boutique capsule hotel located in the heart of Singapore's historic Kampong Glam neighbourhood. - Stay in sleek and modern capsules equipped with personal TVs, power sockets, and reading lights. - Relax and unwind in the hotel's rooftop garden and lounge area, perfect for enjoying the city skyline and meeting fellow visitors.

Mid-Range Accommodations:

1. Hotel Mono: - Immerse yourself in Singapore's rich history at Hotel Mono, a stylish boutique hotel located in the historic Chinatown district. - Stay in beautifully designed rooms featuring sleek monochrome interiors and modern amenities. - Explore the vibrant neighbourhood of Chinatown with its bustling street markets, traditional eateries, and historic sites.

2. Lloyd's Inn: - Experience tranquillity in the heart of the city at Lloyd's Inn, a stylish boutique hotel set in Singapore's Orchard Road neighbourhood. - Relax in simple yet stylish rooms and suites with sleek modern design and thoughtful amenities. - Enjoy the hotel's tranquil garden and rooftop terrace, great for relaxation and unwinding after a day of exploring the city.

Luxury Accommodations:

1. Marina Bay Sands: - Experience luxury at its best at Marina Bay Sands, Singapore's most iconic hotel. -

Enjoy stunning views of the city skyline from the hotel's infinity pool, the world's biggest rooftop pool. - Indulge in world-class dining at one of the hotel's famous chef restaurants, including CUT by Wolfgang Puck and LAVO Italian Restaurant & Rooftop Bar.

2. The Ritz-Carlton, Millenia Singapore: - Treat yourself to a luxury stay at The Ritz-Carlton, Millenia Singapore.
- Relax and unwind in large and elegant rooms and suites with stunning views of Marina Bay.
- Indulge in fine dining experiences at the hotel's award-winning restaurants, including Summer Pavilion and

Chapter 5

Sightseeing and Attractions

Singapore is a vibrant city-state bursting with culture, history, and energy. From iconic landmarks to hidden gems, there's something for everyone to explore and discover in this dynamic city. Here are some of the top sightseeing sites that you won't want to miss during your visit to Singapore:

1. Marina Bay Sands: - Marvel at the stunning design of Marina Bay Sands, one of Singapore's most iconic landmarks. - Take a ride to the top of the hotel's towering viewing deck for breathtaking panoramic views of the city skyline. - Relax and unwind by the hotel's famous infinity pool, the world's biggest rooftop pool, with sweeping views of Marina Bay.

2. Gardens by the Bay: - Immerse yourself in nature at Gardens by the Bay, a sprawling garden oasis set in the heart of the city.

- Explore the iconic Supertree Grove, where towering tree-like structures come to life with a dazzling show of lights and sound every evening.

- Don't miss the chance to visit the Flower Dome and Cloud Forest, two massive conservatories housing thousands of plant types from around the world.

3. Sentosa Island: - Escape the hustle and bustle of the city and relax on the clean beaches of Sentosa Island. - Discover thrilling sites such as Universal Studios Singapore, S.E.A. Aquarium, Adventure Cove Waterpark, and more.

- Enjoy panoramic views of the island from the iconic Sentosa Cable Car, which offers stunning vistas of the city skyline and nearby islands.

4. Chinatown: - Step back in time and explore Singapore's rich Chinese history in the vibrant neighbourhood of Chinatown. - Discover colourful heritage shophouses, bustling street markets, and an array of traditional Chinese churches and shrines. - Don't miss the chance to taste authentic Chinese cuisine at one of Chinatown's many hawker stalls, traditional eateries, or trendy restaurants.

5. Little India: - Experience the sights, sounds, and smells of India in Singapore's lively Little India neighbourhood. - Explore bustling streets lined with coloured shops, aromatic spice stalls, and traditional Indian eateries. - Visit historic sites such as the Sri Veeramakaliamman Temple and the bustling Mustafa Centre, a 24-hour shopping mall that sells everything from electronics to textiles to groceries.

6. Singapore Zoo and Night Safari: - Get up close and personal with wildlife from around the world at the Singapore Zoo and Night Safari. - Explore lush habitats and immersive shows showing animals such as lions, tigers, elephants, and more.

- Experience the magic of the Night Safari, the world's first nocturnal wildlife park, where you can see nocturnal animals in their natural environments under the cover of darkness.

7. Singapore Botanic Gardens: - Discover the beauty of nature at the Singapore Botanic Gardens, a UNESCO World Heritage Site. - Explore lush greenery, colourful blooms, and peaceful lakes and ponds spread across 82 hectares of land. - Don't miss the chance to visit the

National Orchid Garden, home to over 1,000 types and 2,000 hybrids of orchids, including Singapore's national flower, the Vanda Miss Joaquim.

Marina Bay Sands

Marina Bay Sands stands as an iconic symbol of modern Singapore, a marvel of building, luxury, and entertainment that dominates the city's skyline. Here's why Marina Bay Sands should be at the top of your must-visit list:

1. The SkyPark: - Perched 200 metres above ground, the SkyPark offers stunning panoramic views of Singapore's skyline and the bustling Marina Bay.

- Relax by the world's biggest rooftop infinity pool, a stunning architectural feat that offers an unparalleled swimming experience with unmatched views. - Enjoy a leisurely stroll along the SkyPark's viewing deck and take in the stunning vistas of the city, including landmarks such as Gardens by the Bay, the Singapore Flyer, and the iconic Merlion statue.

2. Dining and Nightlife: - Marina Bay Sands is home to a

diverse range of dining choices, from Michelin-starred restaurants to casual eateries.

- Indulge in world-class cuisine at famous chef restaurants such as CUT by Wolfgang Puck, LAVO Italian Restaurant & Rooftop Bar, and Spago Dining Room by Wolfgang Puck. - Experience Singapore's lively nightlife scene at the hotel's and lounges, where you can enjoy craft cocktails, and stunning views of the city skyline.

3. The Shoppes at Marina Bay Sands:

- Shop til you drop at The Shoppes at Marina Bay Sands, a luxury shopping destination offering over 170 premium and designer brands.

- Discover a wide range of foreign and local brands, including iconic fashion houses, luxury boutiques, and unique specialty stores. - Take a leisurely stroll along the picturesque canal and enjoy the hotel's stunning architecture and design, including the famous Louis Vuitton Island Maison and the breathtaking Crystal Pavilion.

4. Entertainment and Attractions: - Marina Bay Sands offers a wealth of entertainment choices for visitors of all

ages.

- Experience world-class entertainment at the Sands Theatre, where you can catch Broadway musicals, foreign concerts, and dazzling stage productions.

- Test your luck at the sprawling casino, which includes a wide range of table games, slot machines, and electronic gaming machines.

5. ArtScience Museum: - Immerse yourself in the world of art and science at the ArtScience Museum, a cutting-edge culture institution located within Marina Bay Sands.

- Explore a varied range of exhibitions and installations showcasing art, science, design, and technology.

- Don't miss the chance to visit famous exhibitions such as Future World: Where Art Meets Science and Wonderland, which feature immersive digital art installations and interactive exhibits.

6. Accommodation: - Experience luxury and comfort in one of Marina Bay Sands' large and elegantly appointed rooms and suites. - Enjoy stunning views of the city skyline, the Marina Bay, or the famous Gardens by the Bay from your room's floor-to-ceiling windows. - Relax

and unwind in luxury amenities, including plush bedding, marble bathrooms, and state-of-the-art entertainment systems.

Marina Bay Sands is more than just a hotel; it's a destination in itself, giving unparalleled luxury, entertainment, and dining experiences that will leave you breathless. Whether you're relaxing by the rooftop infinity pool, indulging in world-class cuisine, or exploring the hotel's many attractions, Marina Bay Sands offers an unforgettable experience that will make your visit to Singapore truly memorable.

Sentosa Island

Nestled just off the southern coast of Singapore, Sentosa Island is a tropical paradise that offers a world of fun, entertainment, and adventure for visitors of all ages. From pristine beaches to thrilling activities, there's something for everyone to enjoy on this idyllic island getaway. Here's why Sentosa Island should be at the top of your must-visit list:

1. Theme Parks and Attractions:
- Sentosa Island is home to some of Singapore's most exciting sites, including Universal Studios Singapore, S.E.A. Aquarium, Adventure Cove Waterpark, and more.
- Experience the magic of Universal Studios Singapore, where you can step into the worlds of your favourite movies and TV shows, including Jurassic Park, Transformers, and Shrek.
- Dive into an underwater world at the S.E.A. Aquarium, home to over 100,000 marine animals from around the world, including sharks, rays, and dolphins.
2. Beaches and Water Sports:
- Relax and unwind on the island's pristine beaches, where you can soak up the sun, swim in crystal-clear waters, and enjoy stunning views of the nearby coastline.
- Try your hand at a wide range of water sports and activities, including kayaking, stand-up paddleboarding, jet skiing, and flying.
- Explore underwater wonders with snorkelling and

diving trips, where you can discover colourful coral reefs, exotic fish, and other marine life.

3. Sentosa Cable Car:

- Take a scenic ride on the Sentosa Cable Car and enjoy amazing views of the island, the city skyline, and the surrounding sea.

- Choose from a variety of cable car experiences, including the Mount Faber Line, the Sentosa Line, and the Sentosa Skyride, each offering a unique view of the island.

- Don't miss the chance to ride the Singapore Cable Car Sky Network at night, when the city lights up and the views are even more amazing.

4. Resorts and Spas:

- Sentosa Island is home to a wide range of luxury resorts and spas, where you can relax, rejuvenate, and enjoy yourself in style.

- Treat yourself to a luxurious spa treatment at one of the island's many world-class spas, where you can engage in massages, facials, and body treatments inspired by traditional Asian healing techniques. - Stay in style at one of Sentosa's luxurious resorts, where you can enjoy roomy accommodations, stunning ocean views, and a wide range of amenities and activities.

5. Dining and Entertainment:

- Sentosa Island offers a diverse range of dining choices, from casual beachfront cafes to fine dining restaurants and trendy bars.

- Enjoy a wide range of cuisines, including Asian, Western, and foreign favourites, served in stunning waterfront settings with panoramic views of the island. - Experience world-class entertainment at Sentosa's many theatres, concert venues, and nightlife hotspots, where you can catch live shows, music concerts, and other exciting events.

6. Eco-Adventure and Nature Parks:

- Explore the island's lush greenery and natural beauty at sites such as the Sentosa Nature Discovery, Butterfly Park & Insect Kingdom, and Fort Siloso Skywalk.

- Discover unique ecosystems, rare plant species, and unusual wildlife as you explore the island's many nature trails and conservation areas.

- Learn about the island's rich history and heritage at historical sites such as Fort Siloso, a former British military fort that offers stunning views of the surrounding coastline.

Sentosa Island is more than just a tropical paradise; it's a world of fun, adventure, and excitement waiting to be discovered. Whether you're relaxing on the beach, exploring thrilling attractions, or enjoying world-class dining and entertainment, Sentosa Island offers an unforgettable experience that will make your visit to Singapore truly memorable.

Gardens by the Bay

Gardens by the Bay is a breathtaking horticultural wonderland that has quickly become one of Singapore's most iconic and must-visit sites. Located in the heart of the city, this award-winning garden attraction spans 101 hectares and features a stunning array of plants, flowers, and architectural wonders. Here's why Gardens by the Bay should be at the top of your must-visit list:

1. Supertree Grove: - The Supertree Grove is perhaps the the most iconic feature of Gardens by the Bay, with its towering tree-like structures that come to life with a dazzling show of lights and sound every evening.

- Marvel at the Supertrees' striking design, which includes vertical gardens that are home to over 162,900 plants from more than 200 kinds.

- Don't miss the chance to take a stroll along the OCBC Skyway, a 128-metre-long walkway that offers stunning panoramic views of the nearby gardens and skyline.

2. Flower Dome and Cloud Forest: - Step into the Flower Dome and Cloud Forest, two massive conservatories that house thousands of plant types from around the world. - Explore the Flower Dome, the world's biggest glass greenhouse, which features a stunning collection of plants and flowers from Mediterranean and semi-arid regions. - Journey through the Cloud Forest, a mysterious world shrouded in mist and home to the world's biggest indoor waterfall, as well as a diverse range of tropical plants and flowers.

3. History Gardens: - Discover the rich cultural history of Singapore at the Heritage Gardens, which feature four

themed gardens inspired by different cultural traditions.

- Explore the Chinese Garden, which displays traditional Chinese landscape design and architecture, including pavilions, bridges, and rockeries.

- Wander through the Malay Garden, which celebrates the rich flora and fauna of Southeast Asia with lush tropical greenery and traditional Malay architecture.

4. Supertree Observatory: - Get a bird's eye view of Gardens by the Bay and the surrounding cityscape from the Supertree Observatory, set atop one of the tallest Supertrees. - Enjoy stunning panoramic views of the city skyline, the Marina Bay, and the nearby gardens from the observatory's indoor and outdoor viewing decks. - Learn about the history, design, and sustainability aspects of Gardens by the Bay through interactive exhibits and displays.

5. Events and Activities: - Gardens by the Bay hosts a wide range of events and activities throughout the year, including floral displays, art exhibitions, music, and festivals. - Don't miss the chance to visit during one of the garden's signature events, such as the Orchid Extravaganza, the Mid-Autumn Festival, or the Sakura

Matsuri.

6. Sustainability and Conservation: - Gardens by the Bay is committed to sustainability and conservation, with a focus on environmental education, research, and conservation activities.

- Learn about the garden's innovative sustainability features, including energy-efficient cooling systems, rainwater harvesting, and solar power generation. - Discover the garden's efforts to conserve and protect endangered plant species through study, propagation, and conservation programs.

Gardens by the Bay is more than just a garden; it's a beautiful green oasis that offers a world of beauty, wonder, and inspiration. Whether you're marvelling at the Supertrees, exploring the conservatories, or learning about sustainability and conservation, Gardens by the Bay offers an unforgettable experience that will leave you inspired and amazed.

Off the beaten path Attractions

While Singapore is known for its iconic landmarks and popular attractions, the city-state is also home to a wealth of hidden gems and secret treasures waiting to be found by intrepid travellers. From hidden enclaves and historic neighbourhoods to quirky museums and offbeat attractions, here are some off the beaten path attractions that you won't find in your normal travel guide:

1. Kampong Buangkok: - Step back in time and explore the last living kampong (traditional village) on mainland Singapore. - Wander through the narrow lanes and rustic houses of Kampong Buangkok, which offer a glimpse into Singapore's country past. - Discover the village's lovely wooden houses, lush gardens, and friendly residents, who are happy to share stories about life in the kampong.

2. Haw Par Villa: - Explore the quirky and surreal world of Haw Par Villa, a theme park that shows Chinese mythology and folklore.

- Marvel at the park's colourful and elaborate sculptures, which represent scenes from classic Chinese tales such as Journey to the West and Romance of the Three Kingdoms. - Don't miss the chance to walk through the park's famous Ten Courts of Hell, a gruesome picture of the afterlife that is sure to leave a lasting impression.

3. The Southern Ridges: - Escape the hustle and bustle of the city and explore the lush greenery of the Southern Ridges, a network of interconnected parks and nature areas.

- Take a leisurely stroll along the Henderson Waves, a stunning pedestrian bridge that offers panoramic views of the nearby forests and coastline. - Discover hidden gems such as the Forest Walk and Canopy Walk, which take you through dense rainforest and offer chances to spot local wildlife such as monkeys and birds.

4. Bukit Brown Cemetery: - Discover Singapore's rich history and heritage at Bukit Brown Cemetery, one of the island's oldest and biggest cemeteries.

- Wander through the cemetery's overgrown pathways and discover its historic graves and tombstones, which date back to the 19th century. - Join a guided tour of the cemetery to learn about its significance and the stories of some of Singapore's early pioneers and important figures.

5. Gillman Barracks: - Immerse yourself in Singapore's modern art scene at Gillman Barracks, a former military barracks that has been turned into a vibrant arts and cultural precinct. - Explore the galleries and art spaces housed in the historic colonial-era buildings, which showcase a diverse range of contemporary art from both local and foreign artists. - Don't miss the chance to attend one of the precinct's regular art shows, events, and performances, which celebrate creativity and innovation in the arts.

6. Pulau Ubin: - Escape the urban jungle and discover the rustic charm of Pulau Ubin, a small island located off the northeastern coast of Singapore. - Discover traditional kampong houses, lush mangrove woods, and pristine beaches as you explore the island by bike or on foot. - Don't miss the chance to visit Chek Jawa Wetlands, a unique ecosystem that is home to a wide range of plant and animal species, including mangroves, seagrasses, and horseshoe crabs.

Singapore is full of hidden gems and secret treasures waiting to be found by intrepid travellers. Whether you're exploring historic neighbourhoods, quirky museums, or lush nature reserves, Singapore's off the beaten path sites promise an unforgettable experience that will leave you inspired and amazed. So step off the tourist trail and find the hidden side of Singapore for yourself!

Museums and Cultural Sites

While Singapore is known for its modern skyline and vibrant city life, the island-state also boasts a rich cultural heritage that is ready to be explored. From world-class museums to historic buildings and cultural sites, there's something for every history buff and culture enthusiast to discover in Singapore. Here are some of the top museums and cultural places that you won't want to miss:

1. National Museum of Singapore: - Step into the past and explore Singapore's rich history and tradition at the National Museum of Singapore, the country's oldest museum. - Discover interactive exhibits, immersive multimedia installations, and artefacts that trace Singapore's trip from its early days as a fishing town to its present-day status as a modern metropolis. - Don't miss the chance to visit the museum's iconic Singapore History Gallery, which shows the island's history through a series of themed galleries and multimedia displays.

2. Peranakan Museum: - Immerse yourself in the vibrant culture and heritage of the Peranakan people at the Peranakan Museum.

- Explore the museum's vast collection of Peranakan artefacts, including traditional costumes, jewellery, furniture, and ceramics.

- Learn about the unique customs, practices, and cuisine of the Peranakan people, who are descendants of Chinese immigrants who settled in Southeast Asia.

3. Asian Civilisations Museum: - Discover the rich cultural diversity of Asia at the Asian Civilisations Museum, which shows the art, artefacts, and heritage of

the region's diverse cultures and civilizations. - Explore the museum's vast collection of artefacts from China, Southeast Asia, South Asia, and the Islamic world, including ceramics, textiles, sculptures, and religious artefacts. - Don't miss the chance to visit the museum's special exhibitions, which feature changing displays of art and artefacts from around the world.

4. ArtScience Museum: - Explore the intersection of art, science, and technology at the ArtScience Museum, a cutting-edge cultural centre located within Marina Bay Sands.

- Discover a wide range of interactive exhibits and installations that explore topics such as creativity, innovation, and sustainability.

- Don't miss the chance to visit famous exhibitions such as Future World: Where Art Meets Science and Wonderland, which feature immersive digital art installations and interactive exhibits.

5. Changi Chapel and Museum: - Learn about the dark days of World War II and the Japanese rule of Singapore at the Changi Chapel and Museum.

- Explore the museum's collection of artefacts, photographs, and personal stories that document the experiences of prisoners of war and civilian internees during this turbulent time in Singapore's past.

- Visit the replica chapel, which was made by prisoners of war during their internment in Changi Prison, and pay your respects to the thousands who lost their lives during this time.

6. Malay Heritage Centre: - Discover the rich cultural heritage of Singapore's Malay people at the Malay Heritage Centre. - Explore the museum's collection of artefacts, textiles, and traditional crafts that showcase the history, culture, and contributions of the Malay people to Singapore's multicultural society. - Don't miss the chance to visit the museum's beautifully renovated heritage buildings, which include a former palace and the historic Istana Kampong Glam.

From ancient artefacts to modern art installations, Singapore's museums and cultural sites offer a fascinating glimpse into the island-state's rich and diverse history. Whether you're interested in history, art, or culture, there's something for everyone to discover in Singapore's bustling cultural scene. So pack your bags and get ready to explore the island's rich history for yourself!

Chapter 6

Activities and Experiences

Singapore is a city-state that offers a wide range of activities and experiences for travellers of all ages and hobbies. From thrilling adventures to cultural experiences and family-friendly attractions, there's something for everyone to enjoy in this vibrant and dynamic city. Here are some of the top events and experiences that you won't want to miss during your visit to Singapore:

1. Night Safari: - Experience the magic of the Night Safari, the world's first nighttime wildlife park. - Embark on a tram ride through seven geographical regions of the world, where you can meet over 2,500 nocturnal animals, including tigers, lions, and elephants. - Explore walking paths that take you through different habitats, such as the Wallaby Trail, Fishing Cat Trail, and Leopard Trail, where you can see animals up close in their naturalistic habitats.

2. Singapore Zoo: - Get up close and personal with wildlife from around the world at the Singapore Zoo. - Explore lush habitats and immersive exhibits that highlight animals such as orangutans, giraffes, and white tigers. - Don't miss the chance to experience unique animal encounters and feeding sessions, where you can learn more about the zoo's residents from experienced keepers.

3. River Safari: - Embark on a trip along the world's most iconic rivers at the River Safari, Asia's first and only river-themed wildlife park. - Explore themed exhibits such as the Amazon Flooded Forest, Giant Panda Forest, and Wild Amazonia, where you can meet a diverse range of river-dwelling animals, including giant otters, manatees, and jaguars. - Take a relaxing boat ride along the Amazon River Quest and the River Safari Cruise, where you can spot exotic wildlife and learn about the value of river conservation.

4. Universal Studios Singapore: - Step into the world of movies and fun at Universal Studios Singapore, Southeast Asia's only Universal Studios theme park. - Explore themed zones such as Hollywood, New York,

Sci-Fi City, and Ancient Egypt, where you can experience exciting rides, attractions, and live shows based on blockbuster movies and TV shows. - Don't miss the chance to meet your favourite characters such as Shrek, Transformers, and the Minions, who make regular visits throughout the park.

5. Adventure Cove Waterpark: - Cool off from the tropical heat at Adventure Cove Waterpark, Singapore's ultimate water playground. - Experience thrilling water slides, rides, and sights such as the Riptide Rocket, Pipeline Plunge, and Rainbow Reef, where you can snorkel with thousands of colourful fish. - Relax and unwind at Bluewater Bay, a tranquil wave pool, or drift along the Adventure River, a lazy river that takes you on a beautiful journey through the park.

6. Sentosa Island: - Escape the hustle and bustle of the city and relax on the clean beaches of Sentosa Island. - Discover thrilling sites such as Universal Studios Singapore, S.E.A. Aquarium, Adventure Cove Waterpark, and more.

- Enjoy panoramic views of the island from the iconic

Sentosa Cable Car, which offers stunning vistas of the city skyline and nearby islands.

7. Gardens by the Bay: - Explore the lush greenery and stunning architecture of Gardens by the Bay, Singapore's iconic garden site.

- Marvel at the Supertree Grove, a collection of towering tree-like structures that come to life with a dazzling show of lights and sound every evening. - Discover the Flower Dome and Cloud Forest, two massive conservatories that house thousands of plant types from around the world.

8. Marina Bay Sands SkyPark: - Take in panoramic views of the city skyline from the Marina Bay Sands SkyPark, a rooftop viewing deck located 200 metres above ground. - Relax by the world's largest rooftop infinity pool, which gives stunning views of Marina Bay.

- Enjoy world-class dining and entertainment choices at Marina Bay Sands, including celebrity chef restaurants, bars, lounges, and a casino.

Shopping Districts

Singapore is renowned for its diverse and vibrant retail scene, offering tourists a shopping experience like no other. From luxury shops and designer labels to bustling street markets and trendy boutiques, there's something for every shopper to discover in this dynamic city-state. Here's a guide to some of the top shopping areas in Singapore:

1. Orchard Road:
- Orchard Road is Singapore's premier shopping area, lined with upscale malls, designer boutiques, and department stores.
- Explore iconic shopping centres such as ION Orchard, Ngee Ann City, and Paragon, which house luxury names like Louis Vuitton, Prada, and Gucci. - Discover unique finds at Orchard Road's specialty stores, including local designers, artisanal crafts, and trendy fashion brands.
2. Marina Bay Sands Shoppes:

- Shop in style at Marina Bay Sands Shoppes, a luxury shopping mall set within the iconic Marina Bay Sands integrated resort.

- Explore a wide range of foreign and designer brands, including Chanel, Dior, and Burberry, as well as exclusive boutiques and flagship stores. - Enjoy stunning waterfront views and world-class dining options as you shop till you drop in this upscale shopping destination.

3. Bugis Street:

- Immerse yourself in the lively atmosphere of Bugis Street, one of Singapore's most famous street markets.

- Browse through hundreds of stalls offering everything from fashion apparel and accessories to gadgets, souvenirs, and street food. - Don't miss the chance to bargain for great deals and unique finds at this bustling shopping area, which is popular with both locals and tourists alike.

4. Haji Lane:

- Explore the eclectic shops and stores of Haji Lane, a colourful and quirky shopping street in Singapore's Arab Quarter.

- Discover unique fashion finds, vintage gems, and

handmade crafts at the street's hip and trendy boutiques. - Enjoy the street's vibrant street art and Instagram-worthy backdrops as you shop, eat, and explore this charming neighbourhood.

5. Chinatown:

- Dive into Singapore's rich cultural history at Chinatown, a bustling neighbourhood known for its vibrant street markets and traditional shophouses. - Explore the busy streets of Chinatown Complex and People's Park Complex, where you can find a wide range of goods, from souvenirs and trinkets to traditional Chinese herbs and spices. - Don't miss the chance to visit the iconic Chinatown Heritage Centre, which offers insights into the history, culture, and customs of Singapore's Chinese community.

6. Little India:

- Experience the sights, sounds, and smells of India in Singapore's lively Little India neighbourhood. - Explore the busy streets of Serangoon Road and Tekka Centre, where you can find a wide range of goods, including textiles, jewellery, spices, and traditional Indian sweets. - Discover unique finds at Little India's specialty shops and boutiques, which offer everything from Bollywood DVDs to intricate handcrafted items.

Dining and Street Food Experiences

Singapore is a melting pot of cultures, and nowhere is this more obvious than in its diverse and vibrant culinary scene. From Michelin-starred fine dining places to bustling hawker centres and street food stalls, Singapore offers a culinary experience like no other. Here's a guide to some of the top dining and street food events that you won't want to miss during your visit:

1. Hawker Centers:
- Dive into Singapore's food culture at its famous hawker centres, where you can find a wide range of affordable and delicious local dishes.
- Explore famous hawker centres such as Maxwell Food Centre, Chinatown Complex, and Lau Pa Sat, where you can sample Singaporean classics like chicken rice, laksa, and chilli crab.

- Don't miss the chance to try Michelin-recommended shops and hawker stalls with long queues, as they often serve some of the best food in the city.

2. Michelin-Starred Dining:

- Indulge in world-class cuisine at Singapore's Michelin-starred restaurants, where you can experience the best of foreign and local flavours.

- Explore acclaimed places such as Liao Fan Hawker Chan, Burnt Ends, and Odette, which have been recognized for their culinary excellence by the prestigious Michelin Guide. - Enjoy innovative and creative dishes made by some of the world's top chefs, and experience Singapore's vibrant dining scene at its best.

3. Peranakan food:

- Experience the unique flavours of food, a fusion of Chinese, Malay, and Indonesian influences. - Explore traditional Peranakan restaurants such as Blue Ginger, Candlenut, and True Blue Cuisine, where you can taste dishes like ayam buah keluak, laksa, and kueh pie tee. - Don't miss the chance to try kueh and desserts, which are known for their intricate designs and delicious tastes.

4. Street Food shops:

- Discover the best of Singapore's street food at its many hawker shops and food markets. - Explore popular food streets such as Jalan Alor, Geylang Serai, and Chinatown Food Street, where you can find a wide range of local and foreign delicacies. - Don't miss the chance to try Singaporean favourites like char kway teow, roti prata, and satay, as well as foreign dishes like Middle Eastern kebabs, Thai mango sticky rice, and Indonesian nasi goreng.

5. Seafood Restaurants:

- Enjoy fresh and flavorful seafood at Singapore's many seafood restaurants, which offer a wide range of meals from the sea.

- Explore seafood spots such as Jumbo Seafood, No Signboard Seafood, and Long Beach Seafood, where you can enjoy Singaporean chilli crab, black pepper crab, and salted egg prawns.

- Don't miss the chance to try other seafood dishes like grilled fish, seafood hotpot, and seafood noodles, which are popular among locals and tourists alike.

6. Food Tours:

- Embark on a culinary adventure with a food tour of Singapore's different neighbourhoods and food markets.

- Explore local favourites and hidden gems with knowledgeable guides who can take you off the beaten path and show you to the best of Singaporean cuisine. - Don't miss the chance to learn about the history, culture, and traditions of Singapore's food culture as you taste a wide range of delicious dishes from all over the world.

Nightlife and Entertainment Options

When the sun goes down, Singapore comes alive with a lively nightlife scene that offers something for everyone. From rooftop bars and nightclubs to live music venues and cultural performances, there's no lack of excitement and entertainment to be found in the Lion City after dark. Here's a guide to some of the top nightlife and entertainment choices that you won't want to miss during your visit:

1. Clarke Quay:

- Experience the heart of Singapore's nightlife scene at Clarke Quay, a bustling riverside area lined with bars, restaurants, and nightclubs. - Explore iconic nightlife spots such as Zouk, Attica, and Canvas, where you can dance the night away to the hottest beats from top DJs and live bands. - Enjoy stunning waterfront views and a wide range of dining options as you explore Clarke Quay's lively nightlife scene.

2. Marina Bay Sands:

- Take in amazing views of the city skyline from the rooftop bars and lounges at Marina Bay Sands.

- Enjoy cocktails and panoramic views at famous rooftop destinations such as CE LA VI, LAVO, and Spago, which offer stunning vistas of the Marina Bay and city skyline. - Experience world-class entertainment at Marina Bay Sands, which hosts regular concerts, theatre productions, and events at its famous Sands Theatre and Grand Theatre.

3. Orchard Road:

- Explore the vibrant nightlife of Orchard Road, Singapore's main shopping and entertainment district. -

Discover hip rooftop bars, stylish lounges, and chic nightclubs such as 1-Altitude, Bar Canary, and The Other Room, where you can enjoy cocktails and live music late into the night. - Don't miss the chance to catch a live performance or concert at one of Orchard Road's many entertainment venues, which host a wide range of local and foreign artists.

4. Sentosa Island:

- Escape the hustle and bustle of the city and party the night away on Sentosa Island, Singapore's top island resort destination. - Discover beachfront bars and clubs such as Tanjong Beach Club, Bikini Bar, and FOC Sentosa, where you can enjoy cocktails, live music, and beautiful sunset views.

- Experience world-class entertainment at Sentosa's many theatres, concert venues, and nightlife hotspots, where you can catch live shows, music concerts, and other exciting events.

5. Cultural Performances:

- Immerse yourself in Singapore's rich cultural history with a traditional dance or music performance. - Explore cultural venues such as the Esplanade - Theatres on the

Bay, the Singapore Chinese Cultural Centre, and the Malay Heritage Centre, which host regular performances and events showcasing traditional and modern arts and culture. - Don't miss the chance to experience traditional performances such as Chinese opera, Indian dance, Malay music, and more, as well as contemporary performances by local and foreign artists.

6. Night Markets:

- Explore Singapore's lively night markets and bazaars, where you can shop for unique gifts, souvenirs, and local handicrafts.

- Discover popular night markets such as the Geylang Serai Bazaar, the Chinatown Night Market, and the Bugis Street Night Market, which offer a wide range of goods, from fashion clothing and accessories to electronics, souvenirs, and street food. - Enjoy live music, cultural shows, and street entertainment as you browse through the stalls and soak up the vibrant atmosphere of Singapore's night markets.

Chapter 7

Cultural Insights

Singapore's cultural landscape is as diverse as its people, with influences from Chinese, Malay, Indian, and Western traditions shaping the island's unique identity. As you discover this vibrant city-state, you'll meet a rich tapestry of customs, traditions, and cultural practices that reflect its multicultural heritage. Here are some cultural insights to help you better understand and respect Singapore's rich and diverse culture:

1. Harmony in Diversity:
 - One of the most striking aspects of Singapore's cultural environment is its harmonious blend of different ethnicities, religions, and cultures.
- Explore areas such as Chinatown, Little India, and Kampong Glam, where you can see mosques, temples, and churches standing side by side, a testament to Singapore's commitment to multiculturalism and religious tolerance. - Don't miss the chance to experience

festivals such as Chinese New Year, Hari Raya Puasa, Deepavali, and Christmas, which are marked with great enthusiasm and joy by Singapore's diverse communities.

2. Peranakan Culture:

- Discover the unique culture and heritage of the Peranakan people, descendants of Chinese immigrants who settled in Southeast Asia and married local Malays.

- Explore the colourful and lively Peranakan architecture of neighbourhoods such as Katong and Joo Chiat, where you can find beautifully preserved shophouses adorned with intricate carvings and colourful tiles.

- Don't miss the chance to try food, a delicious fusion of Chinese, Malay, and Indonesian flavours, which includes dishes such as ayam buah keluak, laksa, and kueh pie tee.

3. Traditional Arts and Crafts:

- Explore Singapore's rich history of arts and crafts, which includes traditional practices such as pottery, weaving, and batik.

- Visit cultural institutions such as the Asian Civilisations Museum, the Malay history Centre, and the Peranakan Museum, where you can learn about

Singapore's cultural history and see examples of traditional arts and crafts.

- Don't miss the chance to buy handmade crafts and souvenirs from local artisans and craftsmen, who sell their wares at markets and shops throughout the city.

4. Language and Communication:

- Singapore is a multilingual society, with English, Mandarin, Malay, and Tamil being the country's main languages. - While English is widely spoken and understood, you'll also hear a lively array of languages and dialects spoken on the streets, including Hokkien, Cantonese, and Malay.

- Don't be afraid to try out a few words of the local languages during your stay, as Singaporeans are usually friendly and welcoming to visitors who make an effort to communicate in their native tongue.

5. Traditional Customs and Etiquette:

- Singaporeans place a high value on respect, courtesy, and social harmony, and there are several traditional customs and etiquette practices that tourists should be aware of.

- When visiting someone's home or entering a place of

worship, it's common to remove your shoes before entering.

- When dining with locals, it's polite to wait for the host to invite you to begin eating before you start your meal, and it's customary to leave a small amount of food on your plate to show that you are full.

6. Festivals and Celebrations:

- Singapore is a city that loves to celebrate, and throughout the year, you'll find a wide range of festivals and celebrations taking place.

- Don't miss the chance to experience festivals such as Chinese New Year, where you can watch colourful parades, lion dances, and fireworks displays.

- Explore the lively streets of Little India during Deepavali, the Festival of Lights, where you can see beautiful light displays, shop for traditional Indian clothes and jewellery, and enjoy delicious Indian snacks and sweets.

Singaporean Culture and Customs

Singapore's rich and diverse culture is a reflection of its multicultural heritage, with influences from Chinese, Malay, Indian, and Western traditions shaping the island's unique character. As you discover this vibrant city-state, you'll meet a rich tapestry of customs, traditions, and cultural practices that reflect its multicultural heritage. Here's a guide to learning Singaporean culture and customs:

1. Harmony in Diversity:

 - One of the most striking aspects of Singaporean society is its harmonious blend of different ethnicities, religions, and cultures.

- Explore areas such as Chinatown, Little India, and Kampong Glam, where you can see mosques, temples, and churches standing side by side, a testament to Singapore's commitment to multiculturalism and religious tolerance.

- Don't miss the chance to experience festivals such as Chinese New Year, Hari Raya Puasa, Deepavali, and

Christmas, which are marked with great enthusiasm and joy by Singapore's diverse communities.

2. Food Culture:

- Singaporeans are passionate about food, and the city-state is famous for its diverse and delicious cuisine.

- Explore hawker centres and street food stalls, where you can taste a wide range of local delicacies such as chicken rice, laksa, and chilli crab.

- Don't miss the chance to try food, a delicious fusion of Chinese, Malay, and Indonesian flavours, which includes dishes such as ayam buah keluak, laksa, and kueh pie tee.

3. Language and Communication:

- Singapore is a multilingual society, with English, Mandarin, Malay, and Tamil being the country's main languages. - While English is widely spoken and understood, you'll also hear a lively array of languages and dialects spoken on the streets, including Hokkien, Cantonese, and Malay.

- Don't be afraid to try out a few words of the local languages during your stay, as Singaporeans are usually friendly and welcoming to visitors who make an effort to communicate in their native tongue.

4. Traditional Arts and Crafts:

- Singapore has a rich history of arts and crafts, which includes traditional practices such as pottery, weaving, and batik.

- Visit cultural institutions such as the Asian Civilisations Museum, the Malay history Centre, and the Peranakan Museum, where you can learn about Singapore's cultural history and see examples of traditional arts and crafts.

- Don't miss the chance to buy handmade crafts and souvenirs from local artisans and craftsmen, who sell their wares at markets and shops throughout the city.

5. Traditional Customs and Etiquette:

- Singaporeans place a high value on respect, courtesy, and social harmony, and there are several traditional customs and etiquette practices that tourists should be aware of.

- When visiting someone's home or entering a place of worship, it's common to remove your shoes before entering.

- When dining with locals, it's polite to wait for the host to invite you to begin eating before you start your meal, and it's customary to leave a small amount of food on your plate to show that you are full.

6. Festivals and Celebrations:

- Singapore is a city that loves to celebrate, and throughout the year, you'll find a wide range of festivals and celebrations taking place.

- Don't miss the chance to experience festivals such as Chinese New Year, where you can watch colourful parades, lion dances, and fireworks displays.

- Explore the lively streets of Little India during Deepavali, the Festival of Lights, where you can see beautiful light displays, shop for traditional Indian clothes and jewellery, and enjoy delicious Indian snacks and sweets.

Singaporean culture is a rich tapestry of customs, traditions, and cultural practices that reflect the island's multicultural history. As you explore this vibrant city-state, you'll meet a diverse and dynamic culture that is sure to leave a lasting impression. So come and immerse yourself in the cultural delights of Singapore for an unforgettable experience!

Language Tips

Singapore is a melting pot of cultures, and its multilingual society reflects the varied heritage of its people. While English is the main language of communication, you'll also hear a colourful array of languages and dialects spoken on the streets, including Mandarin, Malay, Tamil, Hokkien, and Cantonese. Here are some language tips to help you manage Singapore's multilingual landscape:

1. English:
- English is widely spoken and understood in Singapore, and it is the main language of communication in schools, businesses, and government organisations.
- Most signs, menus, and public announcements are in English, making it easy for travellers to get around and speak with locals.

- Singaporean English has its own unique vocabulary and grammar, so don't be surprised if you hear phrases like "lah," "lor," and "leh" in everyday talk.

2. Mandarin Chinese:

- Mandarin Chinese is the most regularly spoken language in Singapore after English, and it is widely used in business and commerce.

- While most Singaporeans are skilled in Mandarin, there are also many different dialects of Chinese spoken in the country, including Hokkien, Cantonese, and Teochew. - If you know Mandarin, you'll have no trouble communicating with locals, especially in areas with a large Chinese population such as Chinatown and Orchard Road.

3. Malay:

-Malay is one of Singapore's four official languages, and it is spoken by the Malay people, as well as by many other ethnic groups in the country. - While English is the main language of communication in most situations, you'll still hear Malay spoken in areas such as Kampong Glam and Geylang Serai.

- Learning a few simple Malay phrases such as "Selamat pagi" (Good morning), "Terima kasih" (Thank you), and "Sila" (Please) can go a long way in making a good impression with locals.

4. Tamil:

- Tamil is another one of Singapore's official languages, and it is spoken by the Tamil people, as well as by many other ethnic groups in the country.

- While English is the main language of communication in most situations, you'll still hear Tamil spoken in areas such as Little India and Serangoon Road. - Learning a few basic Tamil phrases such as "Vanakkam" (Hello), "Nandri" (Thank you), and "Ponaal " (Please) can help you connect with locals and make your stay more fun.

5. languages:

- In addition to Mandarin, Malay, and Tamil, there are also several Chinese languages spoken in Singapore, including Hokkien, Cantonese, Teochew, and Hakka.

- While English is the main language of communication in most situations, you'll still hear these dialects spoken in areas such as Chinatown, where they are an important part of the local culture.

- Learning a few basic words in a local dialect such as "Huat ah" (Good luck) in Hokkien, "Lai lai" (Come come) in Cantonese, or "Jiak ba ?" (Have you eaten?) Teochew can help you connect with locals and make your stay more enjoyable.

Navigating Singapore's multilingual world is easy with these language tips. Whether you're speaking in English, Mandarin, Malay, Tamil, or a local dialect, learning a few basic phrases can help you connect with locals and make your stay more enjoyable. So don't be afraid to immerse yourself in Singapore's diverse language and culture during your stay!

Etiquette and Cultural Norms

Singapore is a city-state known for its rich cultural tapestry and diverse people. While it is a modern and cosmopolitan city, it also has its own set of unique customs, practices, and social norms. Understanding and respecting these cultural nuances will not only improve your travel experience but also help you make a positive impression on the locals. Here's a guide to handling Singapore's social landscape:

1. Respect for Diversity:
- Singapore is a melting pot of cultures, with Chinese, Malay, Indian, and Western influences shaping its unique character.
- Respect for diversity is deeply ingrained in Singaporean culture, and tourists are expected to be tolerant and respectful of different ethnicities, religions, and cultural practices.
- Take the time to learn about Singapore's multicultural history and enjoy the rich tapestry of customs, traditions, and cuisines that make the city unique.

2. Greeting Etiquette:
- When meeting someone for the first time, a handshake is the most usual form of greeting in Singapore.
- Addressing someone by their title and surname (e.g., Mr. Tan, Mrs. Lee) is considered polite and respectful, especially in professional settings.

- In Chinese culture, it is customary to call someone by their title followed by their surname (e.g., Ah Meng, Ah Seng) as a sign of respect.

3. Dining Etiquette:

- Singaporeans take their food seriously, and dining is an important social practice in the city-state.

- When dining with locals, wait for the host to ask you to start eating before you begin your meal.

- It is considered nice to try a bit of everything on your plate and to leave a small amount of food as a sign that you are full.

4. Dress Code:

- Singapore is a modern and cosmopolitan city, but it is also a conservative society with strict dress codes in certain situations.

- When visiting temples, mosques, and other places of worship, modest dress is needed, with shoulders and knees covered.

- In business and formal settings, smart casual attire is appropriate, while beachwear and revealing clothing should be kept for the beach or poolside.

5. Public Behaviour:

- Singapore is known for its strict laws and regulations, and tourists are expected to adhere to local customs and social norms.

- Chewing gum is banned in Singapore, and littering, spitting, and smoking in public places are strictly barred.

- While Singapore is a safe city, it is important to be aware of your surroundings and to practise caution, especially when using public transportation or exploring unfamiliar areas.

6. Tipping and Service Charges:

- Tipping is not a popular practice in Singapore, as a 10% service charge is usually included in the bill at restaurants and hotels.

- However, if you receive exceptional service, it is customary to leave a small tip as a token of gratitude.

- In taxis and for other services, rounding up the fare is generally sufficient.

Navigating Singapore's social landscape is easy with these etiquette and cultural rules. By respecting local customs, traditions, and social norms, you'll not only enhance your travel experience but also make a good effect on the locals. So accept the rich cultural tapestry of Singapore and enjoy your time in this vibrant and diverse city-state!

Chapter 8

Day Trips and Excursions

While Singapore has a wealth of sights and experiences to offer within its city limits, there are also plenty of exciting day trips and excursions that allow travellers to explore beyond the bustling metropolis. From lush nature areas and idyllic islands to historic towns and cultural landmarks, there's something for everyone to discover just a short journey away from the Lion City. Here's a guide to some of the best day trips and outings from Singapore:

1. Pulau Ubin:

- Escape the hustle and bustle of the city and trip back in time with a visit to Pulau Ubin, a rustic island located just a short boat ride away from Singapore.

- Explore the island's lush forests, tranquil beaches, and traditional villages by bike or on foot, and discover a way of life that has stayed unchanged for decades.

- Don't miss the chance to visit Chek Jawa Wetlands, a unique ecosystem teeming with wildlife, where you can spot mangrove forests, seagrass lagoons, and coral reefs.

2. Sentosa Island:

- Discover the ultimate playground for fun and relaxation with a day trip to Sentosa Island, Singapore's top island resort destination.

- Relax on pristine beaches, enjoy thrilling sites such as Universal Studios Singapore and S.E.A. Aquarium, and indulge in world-class dining and entertainment options.

- Don't miss the chance to catch a beautiful sunset at Siloso Beach, explore the lush greenery of Fort Siloso, or take a leisurely stroll along the Sentosa Boardwalk.

3. Batam Island, Indonesia:

- Embark on an exciting day trip to Batam Island, just a short ferry ride away from Singapore, and discover the natural beauty and cultural attractions of Indonesia.

- Explore the island's beautiful beaches, lush rainforests, and traditional villages, and enjoy sports such as snorkelling, diving, and kayaking.

- Don't miss the chance to visit Nagoya Hill Shopping Mall, where you can shop for souvenirs, handicrafts, and local delicacies, or rest at a seaside resort and spa.

4. Johor Bahru, Malaysia:

- Cross the border into Malaysia and explore the lively city of Johor Bahru, just a short drive from Singapore.

– Discover cultural landmarks such as Sultan Abu Bakar Mosque and Sultan Ibrahim Building, or visit the bustling streets of Little India and Chinatown.

- Don't miss the chance to indulge in delicious Malaysian cuisine at local eateries and street food stalls, or shop for souvenirs and deals at Johor Bahru's many markets and shopping malls.

5. Malacca, Malaysia:

- Immerse yourself in history and culture with a day trip to Malacca, a UNESCO World Heritage Site located just a few hours' drive from Singapore.

- Explore the city's historic sites and cultural attractions, including A Famosa, St. Paul's Hill, and Jonker Street, where you can shop for antiques, handicrafts, and local delicacies.

- Don't miss the chance to try delicious cuisine at a local restaurant, or take a relaxing cruise along the Malacca River to see the city from a different view.

6. Gardens by the Bay and Marina Barrage:

- Explore Singapore's stunning Gardens by the Bay and Marina Barrage on a day trip that mixes nature, recreation, and breathtaking views.

- Discover the famous Supertree Grove, Flower Dome, and Cloud Forest at Gardens by the Bay, where you can marvel at exotic plants, stunning floral displays, and futuristic architecture. - Don't miss the chance to enjoy a picnic and panoramic views of the city skyline from Marina Barrage, or take a leisurely walk along the waterfront promenade for a relaxing day out.

With so many exciting day trips and excursions to choose from, there's no lack of adventures to be had just a short journey away from Singapore. Whether you're exploring lush nature reserves and idyllic islands, finding historic towns and cultural landmarks, or simply enjoying the stunning views and recreational activities on offer, there's something for everyone to enjoy beyond the bustling metropolis of the Lion City. So pack your bags, embark on an adventure, and find the wonders that lie just beyond Singapore's city limits!

Excursions within Singapore

While Singapore is known for its modern skyline and bustling city life, the island nation also offers a myriad of exciting outings and day trips within its own borders. From tranquil nature reserves and lush gardens to cultural enclaves and historic neighbourhoods, there's a wealth of experiences waiting to be found right here in the Lion City. Here's a guide to some of the most enticing trips within Singapore:

1. MacRitchie Reservoir:
- Escape the urban hustle and bustle with a visit to MacRitchie Reservoir, a peaceful oasis located in the heart of Singapore.
- Explore the reservoir's lush rainforest trails, and start on a scenic hike along the TreeTop Walk, where you can enjoy panoramic views of the surrounding landscape.

- Don't miss the chance to paddle through the tranquil waters of the reservoir on a kayak or canoe, or spot local wildlife such as monkeys, monitor lizards, and exotic birds.

2. Singapore Botanic Gardens:

- Discover the natural beauty and calm of the Singapore Botanic Gardens, a UNESCO World Heritage Site located just minutes from the city centre.

- Explore the garden's lush landscapes, themed gardens, and picturesque lakes, and look at the stunning displays of tropical flora and fauna.

- Don't miss the chance to visit the National Orchid Garden, home to over 1,000 kinds of orchids, including the iconic Singapore orchid.

3. Kampong Glam:

- Immerse yourself in the rich cultural history of Kampong Glam, Singapore's historic Malay quarter.

– Explore the neighbourhood's colourful streets, and visit cultural sites such as the Sultan Mosque, Malay Heritage Centre, and Arab Street.

- Don't miss the chance to shop for traditional textiles, handicrafts, and spices at the busy street markets and boutique shops.

4. Little India:

- Experience the sights, sounds, and flavours of India with a visit to Little India, one of Singapore's most vibrant and colourful areas.

- Explore the area's bustling streets, and visit cultural landmarks such as Sri Veeramakaliamman Temple, Tekka Centre, and Mustafa Centre.

- Don't miss the chance to try delicious Indian cuisine at local eateries and street food stalls, or shop for spices, saris, and souvenirs at the many shops and markets.

5. Chinatown:

- Step back in time with a visit to Chinatown, Singapore's famous Chinese enclave.

- Explore the neighbourhood's bustling streets, and visit cultural sites such as the Buddha Tooth Relic Temple, Thian Hock Keng Temple, and Chinatown Heritage Centre.

- Don't miss the chance to taste authentic Chinese cuisine at local restaurants and street food stalls, or shop for souvenirs, antiques, and traditional Chinese goods at the many shops and markets.

6. Haw Par Villa:

- Discover the quirky and colourful world of Haw Par Villa, a unique theme park that shows Chinese mythology and folklore.

- Explore the park's elaborate statues, dioramas, and displays, and learn about famous Chinese legends such as the Journey to the West and the Romance of the Three Kingdoms.

- Don't miss the chance to take a leisurely walk through the park's landscaped gardens and enjoy panoramic views of the city skyline.

Chapter 9

Practical Information

Before embarking on your journey to Singapore, it's important to have all the practical information you need to make your trip smooth and enjoyable. From visa requirements and currency to transportation and communication, here's everything you need to know to handle the Lion City like a pro:

1. Visa Requirements:

- Most people in Singapore do not require a visa for short stays of up to 30 days.

- Nationals of visa waiver eligible countries can enter Singapore without a visa for tourism, work, or social visits.

- Check the Ministry of Foreign Affairs website for the most up-to-date information on visa requirements and entry rules.

2. Currency:

- The currency used in Singapore is the Singapore Dollar (SGD).

- ATMs are widely available throughout the city, and credit cards are accepted at most hotels, bars, and shops.

- It's a good idea to take some cash for smaller purchases and transactions, especially at local markets and food stalls.

3. Language:

- The official languages of Singapore are English, Mandarin, Malay, and Tamil.

- English is widely spoken and understood, making it easy for travellers to interact with locals.

- Learning a few simple phrases in the local languages, such as "Thank you" (Terima kasih), can be appreciated by locals.

4. Transportation:

- Singapore has an efficient and vast public transportation system, including buses and the MRT (Mass Rapid Transit) system.

- The EZ-Link card or Singapore Tourist Pass allows for unlimited rides on buses and trains for a specified time.

- Taxis and ride-hailing services such as Grab are easily available and can be hailed on the street or booked via mobile apps.

5. Climate:

- Singapore has a tropical jungle climate, with warm and humid weather year-round. - The average temperature runs from 25°C to 31°C (77°F to 88°F), with high humidity levels. - Be sure to pack light, breathable clothes, and carry an umbrella or raincoat for sudden downpours.

6. Safety and Security:

- Singapore is one of the safest places in the world, with low crime rates and strict law enforcement.

- However, it's always a good idea to apply caution and be aware of your surroundings, especially in crowded areas and tourist attractions.

- In case of emergency, dial 999 for police, fire, or medical help.

7. Health and Safety:

- Singapore has great healthcare facilities and medical services.

- Tap water is safe to drink, but bottled water is easily available and widely used.

- It's advisable to apply mosquito repellent, especially in outdoor areas, to avoid mosquito-borne diseases like dengue fever.

8. Electricity:

- Singapore uses the Type G electrical plug, with a common voltage of 230V and a frequency of 50Hz.

- Travellers from countries with different plug types will need a trip adapter to use their electronic devices.

9. Wi-Fi and Communication:

- Free Wi-Fi is offered in many public areas, including shopping malls, cafes, and tourist attractions.

- SIM cards with data plans can be bought at convenience stores, mobile phone shops, and the airport for easy and affordable internet access.

10. Tipping:

- Tipping is not customary in Singapore, as a 10% service charge is usually included in the bill at restaurants and hotels. - However, if you receive exceptional service, a small tip is welcomed but not expected.

Safety Tips

Singapore is known for its safety and security, making it an ideal place for travellers. However, it's always important to prioritise your safety and well-being, no matter where you are in the world. Here are some safety tips to help you enjoy your time in Singapore with peace of mind:

1. Be Aware of Your Surroundings:
- While Singapore is usually safe, it's essential to remain vigilant and aware of your surroundings, especially in crowded tourist areas and public transportation hubs.
 - Keep an eye on your belongings at all times and be careful of pickpockets, especially in crowded places like markets and shopping centres.
2. Stay Hydrated:
- Singapore has a tropical environment with high temperatures and humidity levels year-round.
- Stay hydrated by drinking plenty of water throughout the day, especially if you're out exploring the city on

foot.

3. Use Reliable Transportation:

- Singapore has an excellent public transportation system, including buses and the MRT (Mass Rapid Transit) system.

- Use licensed taxis or reputable ride-hailing services like Grab for extra safety and convenience, especially when travelling late at night.

4. Follow Traffic Rules:

- If you're planning to rent a bicycle or use electric scooters to explore the city, be sure to follow traffic rules and laws.

- Stay in marked bike lanes and pedestrian paths, and always wear a helmet for your safety.

5. Be Cautious with Street Food:

- Singapore is famous for its delicious street food, but it's important to be cautious when trying new dishes from street vendors.

- Choose food stalls that are busy with locals, as this is a sign of fresh and safe food. Avoid stalls with food that has been sitting out for a long time.

6. Protect Yourself from the Sun:

- Singapore's tropical temperature means that the sun can be intense, even on cloudy days. - Wear sunscreen with a high SPF, a wide-brimmed hat, and sunglasses to protect yourself from dangerous UV rays.

7. Be Mindful of Wildlife:

- While Singapore is a modern city, it is also home to a variety of wildlife, including monkeys, monitor lizards, and snakes.

- Keep a safe distance from wildlife and refrain from feeding them, as this can lead to violent behaviour.

8. Use Crosswalks and Pedestrian Crossings:

- Singapore has strict traffic rules, and jaywalking is illegal and can be dangerous.

- Use marked crosswalks and pedestrian crossings when crossing the street, and wait for the signal to indicate that it's safe to cross.

9. Stay Informed:

- Familiarise yourself with emergency contact lines, including the police (999), ambulance (995), and fire department (995).

- Keep your accommodation's address and contact

information ready, as well as the contact information for your country's embassy or consulate in Singapore.

10. believe Your Instincts:

- If something doesn't feel right or you feel uncomfortable in a situation, believe your instincts and remove yourself from the situation.

- Don't hesitate to ask for help or support from locals or authorities if you need it.

Health Information

Ensuring your health and well-being is important when travelling, and Singapore offers excellent healthcare facilities and services to keep you safe during your visit. Here's everything you need to know to stay healthy and aware while exploring the Lion City:

1. Vaccinations and Health Precautions:

- No specific vaccinations are needed for entry into Singapore for most travellers.

- However, it's a good idea to ensure that routine vaccinations such as measles, mumps, rubella (MMR), diphtheria, tetanus, and pertussis (DTaP), and influenza are up to date before going.

- If you're going to visit rural or forested areas, consider getting vaccinated against mosquito-borne diseases like dengue fever and Japanese encephalitis.

2. Drinking Water:

- Tap water in Singapore is safe to drink and meets World Health Organization standards.

- Bottled water is also easily available and widely used, especially for convenience.

3. Food Safety:

- Singapore is known for its diverse and delicious cuisine, but it's important to be cautious about food safety.

- Choose food stalls and places with a high turnover of customers, as this is a sign of fresh and safe food.

- Avoid eating raw or undercooked food, and make sure that fruits and vegetables are fully washed and peeled before consumption.

4. Sun Protection:

- Singapore has a tropical environment with high temperatures and humidity levels year-round.

- Protect yourself from the sun by wearing sunscreen with a high SPF, a wide-brimmed hat, and shades.

- Seek shade during the hottest parts of the day, usually between 10:00 AM and 4:00 PM.

5. Mosquito Protection:

- Singapore is also known for its warm and humid weather, which offers an ideal environment for mosquitoes.

- Protect yourself from mosquito bites by wearing long-sleeved shirts and long pants, especially during dawn and dusk when mosquitoes are most active.

- Use bug repellent containing DEET or Picaridin, and consider sleeping under a mosquito net if you're staying in accommodations without air conditioning or screens on windows.

6. Healthcare Facilities:

- Singapore has world-class healthcare facilities and medical services, with hospitals and clinics found throughout the city.

- The Singapore General Hospital and Mount Elizabeth

Hospital are two of the biggest and most well-known hospitals in the country.

- In case of a medical emergency, dial 995 for an ambulance or visit the nearby hospital emergency department.

7. Travel Insurance:

- While healthcare in Singapore is of a high standard, medical treatment can be expensive for visitors without insurance.

- Consider buying travel insurance that includes coverage for medical emergencies, trip cancellations, and lost or stolen belongings.

8. Pharmacies and Medications:

- Pharmacies in Singapore, known as "pharmacies" or "pharmacies," are well-stocked with a wide range of medicines and over-the-counter remedies.

- Common medications such as pain relievers, cold and flu remedies, and allergy medications are easily available.

- Bring a copy of your prescription or a note from your doctor if you're going with prescription medications.

Emergency Contacts

When travelling to Singapore, it's essential to have access to emergency contacts in case you experience any unexpected situations. Here are the important emergency contacts you should know while exploring the Lion City:

1. Police:
- Emergency Number: 999
- The Singapore Police Force is responsible for maintaining law and order, as well as ensuring the safety and protection of residents and visitors.
- Dial 999 to report emergencies such as accidents, crimes, or any other urgent situations needing police assistance.

2. Ambulance and Medical Emergencies:
- Emergency Number: 995
- The Singapore Civil Defence Force (SCDF) operates the ambulance service and reacts to medical emergencies.
- Dial 995 for immediate medical help in case of accidents, injuries, or medical emergencies.

3. Fire and Rescue Services:

- Emergency Number: 995

- The SCDF also offers fire and rescue services in Singapore.

- Dial 995 to report fires, hazardous materials incidents, or any other emergency needing fire and rescue assistance.

4. Non-Emergency Police Assistance:

- Police Hotline: 1800 255 0000

- For non-emergency police help, you can call the police hotline.

- This number can be used to report non-urgent matters, ask advice, or make general inquiries.

5. Tourist Police Hotline:

- Tourist Police Hotline: 1800 736 8679 (1800 736 TOUR) - The Tourist Police Hotline is especially for tourists who require assistance or information while in Singapore.

- This hotline works 24/7 and provides support in multiple languages.

6. Embassy and Consulate Contacts:

- It's important to have the contact information for your country's embassy or consulate in Singapore in case of emergencies or if you require assistance while abroad.

- Here are the contact information for some embassies and consulates in Singapore:

- United States Embassy in Singapore:

- Address: 27 Napier Road, Singapore 258508 - Phone: +65 6476 9100

- Australian High Commission in Singapore: - Address: 25 Napier Road, Singapore 258507 - Phone: +65 6836 4100

- British High Commission in Singapore: - Address: 100 Tanglin Road, Singapore 247919 - Phone: +65 6424 4200

7. Directory Enquiries:

- Directory Enquiries: 100 - If you require contact information for businesses, government bodies, or other organisations in Singapore, you can dial 100 for directory assistance.

8. Foreign Missions and Diplomatic Missions:

- For a comprehensive list of foreign missions and diplomatic missions in Singapore, you can check the Ministry of Foreign Affairs website at www.mfa.gov.sg.

Chapter 10

Useful Resources

When travelling to Singapore, having access to useful tools can enhance your experience and make your trip more enjoyable. From transportation and accommodation to dining and sightseeing, here are some important resources to help you navigate the Lion City with ease:

1. Singapore Tourism Board (STB):
- Website: www.visitsingapore.com
- The Singapore Tourism Board (STB) is the official tourism organisation for Singapore, offering comprehensive information and resources for travellers.
- Visit their website for up-to-date information on sites, events, tours, accommodations, and more.
2. Visit Singapore Mobile App:
- Available on iOS and Android devices - The Visit Singapore mobile app is a handy tool for travellers, offering access to important travel information on the go.

- Use the app to discover attractions, plan your itinerary, find dining choices, book tours, and navigate the city with ease.

3. Public Transportation:

- Website: www.mytransport.sg

- MyTransport.sg is Singapore's official public transportation website, offering information on bus and train services, routes, schedules, and fares.

- Use the website or mobile app to plan your journeys, check real-time arrival information, and travel the city using public transportation.

4. Singapore Maps:

- Website: www.streetdirectory.com

- Streetdirectory.com gives detailed maps of Singapore, including street maps, tourist maps, and interactive maps.

- Use the website or mobile app to find directions, identify attractions, restaurants, hotels, and more.

5. Singapore Airlines:

- Website: www.singaporeair.com

- Singapore Airlines is the national carrier of Singapore, giving flights to destinations around the world. - Visit their website to buy flights, check flight status, manage bookings, and explore travel deals and promotions.

6. Changi Airport:

- Website: www.changiairport.com

- Changi Airport is one of the busiest and most awarded airports in the world, acting as a major hub for international travel.

- Visit their website for information on flights, terminals, buildings, services, and transit choices at Changi Airport.

7. Accommodation Booking Platforms:

- Websites: www.booking.com, www.agoda.com, www.expedia.com

- Booking.com, Agoda, and Expedia are popular accommodation booking platforms, giving a wide choice of hotels, hostels, guesthouses, and serviced apartments in Singapore.

- Use these websites to compare prices, read reviews, and book accommodations that fit your preferences and budget.

8. Food Delivery Services:

- Websites: www.foodpanda.sg, www.deliveroo.com.sg, www.grab.com/sg

- Foodpanda, Deliveroo, and GrabFood are popular food delivery services in Singapore, giving a wide range of cuisines for delivery to your doorstep.

- Use these apps to order food from your favourite restaurants and places, even when you're on the go.

9. Weather Forecast:

- Website: www.weather.gov.sg

- The Meteorological Service Singapore offers up-to-date weather forecasts, warnings, and advisories for Singapore.

- Check their website for the latest weather information to help you plan your activities and trips.

10. Singapore Events and Festivals:

- Website: www.yoursingapore.com/events-calendar - Visit Singapore's events calendar for information on future events, festivals, concerts, exhibitions, and cultural performances in Singapore.

- Plan your trip around exciting events and experiences to make the most of your time in the Lion City.

Websites and Apps

In today's digital age, having access to the right websites and apps can make your trip experience in Singapore seamless and enjoyable. From navigating the city to discovering hidden gems and finding the best dining spots, here are some important websites and apps to enhance your travel experience:

1. Visit Singapore (Website and Mobile App):
- Website: [Visit Singapore](https://www.visitsingapore.com/)
- Mobile App: Visit Singapore (Available on iOS and Android)
- The Visit Singapore website and mobile app are your ultimate guides to discovering the Lion City.
- Discover top attractions, events, dining choices, accommodations, and more.
- Plan your itinerary, book tours, and navigate the city with ease using the interactive map and transportation details.
2. MyTransport.SG (Website and Mobile App):

- Website: [MyTransport.SG](https://www.mytransport.sg/)

- Mobile App: MyTransport.SG (Available on iOS and Android)

- MyTransport.SG is Singapore's main public transportation website and mobile app.

- Plan your journeys using buses and trains, check real-time arrival information, and travel the city with ease.

- Access information on routes, schedules, fares, and transportation updates to make your journey around Singapore hassle-free.

3. Streetdirectory.com (Website and Mobile App):

-Website:[Streetdirectory.com](https://www.streetdirectory.com/)

- Mobile App: Streetdirectory (Available on iOS and Android)

- Streetdirectory.com gives detailed maps of Singapore, including street maps, tourist maps, and interactive maps.

- Find directions, find attractions, restaurants, hotels, and more with ease.

- Access real-time traffic updates, parking information, and public transportation routes to navigate the city effectively.

4. Singapore Airlines (Website and Mobile App):

- Website: [Singapore Airlines](https://www.singaporeair.com/)

- Mobile App: Singapore Airlines (Available on iOS and Android)

- Singapore Airlines is the national carrier of Singapore, offering flights to places around the world.

- Book flights, manage bookings, check flight status, and explore travel deals and promos.

- Access in-flight entertainment, flight information, and airport guides to make your trip experience with Singapore Airlines seamless and enjoyable.

5. Changi Airport (Website and Mobile App):

- Website: [Changi Airport](https://www.changiairport.com/)

- Mobile App: iChangi (Available on iOS and Android)

- Changi Airport is one of the busiest and most awarded airports in the world, acting as a major hub for international travel.

- Access details on flights, terminals, buildings, services, and transit options at Changi Airport.

- Use the iChangi mobile app to navigate the airport, track flights, and explore dining, shopping, and entertainment choices.

6. Booking.com, Agoda, Expedia (Websites and Mobile Apps):

- Websites: [Booking.com](https://www.booking.com/), [Agoda](https://www.agoda.com/), [Expedia](https://www.expedia.com.sg/)

- Mobile Apps: Booking.com, Agoda, Expedia (Available on iOS and Android) - Booking.com, Agoda, and Expedia are popular accommodation booking platforms, giving a wide range of hotels, hostels, guesthouses, and serviced apartments in Singapore.

- Compare prices, read reviews, and book accommodations that suit your tastes and budget with ease.

7. Foodpanda, Deliveroo, GrabFood (Websites and Mobile Apps): - Websites: [Foodpanda](https://www.foodpanda.sg/), [Deliveroo](https://www.deliveroo.com.sg/),

[GrabFood](https://www.grab.com/sg/)
- Mobile Apps: Foodpanda, Deliveroo, GrabFood (Available on iOS and Android) - Foodpanda, Deliveroo, and GrabFood are popular food delivery services in Singapore, giving a wide range of cuisines for delivery to your doorstep.
- Order food from your favourite restaurants and places with ease, even when you're on the go.
8. Weather.gov.sg (Website): -

Website: [Meteorological Service Singapore](https://www.weather.gov.sg/)
- The Meteorological Service Singapore offers up-to-date weather forecasts, warnings, and advisories for Singapore.
- Check the website for the latest weather information to help you plan your activities and trips.

Tour Operators and Travel Agencies

When visiting a vibrant place like Singapore, tour operators and travel agencies can play a crucial role in ensuring that you make the most of your time in the Lion

City. From guided tours and personalised itineraries to hassle-free travel arrangements, these pros can help you create unforgettable experiences. Here's why you should consider using tour operators and travel firms during your trip to Singapore:

1. Expert Local Knowledge:
- Tour operators and travel agencies in Singapore have expert local knowledge, allowing them to create unique and immersive experiences for travellers.
- They know the ins and outs of the city, from hidden gems and local hotspots to the best times to visit famous attractions.

2. Convenience and Ease:
- Planning a trip can be overwhelming, especially when visiting a new location. Tour operators and travel agencies take the hassle out of journey planning by handling all the details for you.
- From arranging transportation and accommodations to booking tours and activities, they ensure that every aspect of your trip is taken care of.

3. Customised Itineraries:

- Tour operators and travel agencies can create customised itineraries tailored to your interests, preferences, and budget. - Whether you're interested in food tours, cultural experiences, outdoor adventures, or shopping excursions, they can design the perfect itinerary to suit your needs.

4. Access to Exclusive Experiences:

- Tour operators and travel agencies often have access to exclusive experiences and VIP treatment that may not be available to independent travellers. - Whether it's a private tour of a museum, a behind-the-scenes look at a local attraction, or a special dining experience, they can help you access the best that Singapore has to offer.

5. Local Guides and Experts:

- Many tour operators employ local guides and experts who are passionate about sharing their knowledge and love for their city.

- These guides provide valuable insights into Singapore's history, culture, and traditions, enhancing your overall travel experience.

6. Safety and Peace of Mind:

- Travelling with a reputable tour operator or travel agency provides an extra layer of safety and peace of mind.

- They have established relationships with trusted vendors and service providers, ensuring that you have a safe and enjoyable experience throughout your trip.

7. Group Tours and Solo Travelers:

- Whether you're travelling solo, with family and friends, or as part of a group, tour operators and travel agencies offer options to suit every traveller.

- Join a group tour to meet like-minded travellers and explore the city together, or opt for a private tour for a more personalised experience.

8. Last-Minute Assistance:

- In the event of any unforeseen circumstances or emergencies during your trip, tour operators and travel agencies are there to provide assistance and support. - They can help you rebook flights, make alternate travel arrangements, or provide guidance and support as needed.

9. Reputable Tour Operators and Agencies in Singapore:
- Some reputable tour operators and travel agencies in Singapore include:
- Singapore Airlines Holidays
- Chan Brothers Travel
- JTB Singapore
- Dynasty Travel
- CTC Travel

Sample Itineraries for Different Lengths of Stay

Whether you have a few days or a week to spend in Singapore, there's plenty to see and do in this lively city-state. To help you make the most of your time, here are example itineraries for different lengths of stay:

1. 2-Day Itinerary: Quick Getaway

Day 1: Explore the City

- Morning: - Start your day with a walk to Gardens by the Bay. Explore the Flower Dome, Cloud Forest, and

Supertree Grove. - Enjoy a relaxed walk along the OCBC Skyway for panoramic views of the city skyline.

- Afternoon: - Head to Chinatown for lunch and discover the bustling streets filled with shops, temples, and street food stalls.

- Visit the Buddha Tooth Relic Temple and Museum, and discover the vibrant neighbourhood of Chinatown.

- Evening: - Take a river cruise along the Singapore River and enjoy the city's iconic landmarks illuminated at night. - End your day with dinner at Clarke Quay, a vibrant riverside dining and entertainment spot.

Day 2: Sentosa Island Adventure

- Morning: - Spend the morning at Sentosa Island. Visit Universal Studios Singapore and enjoy thrilling rides and activities.

- Afternoon: - Have lunch at one of the many places on Sentosa Island.

- Visit S.E.A. Aquarium, home to over 100,000 sea animals, including sharks, rays, and colourful fish.

- Evening: - Relax on the beach or take a leisurely walk along the Sentosa Boardwalk. - Enjoy dinner at one of the waterfront restaurants and watch the sunset over the South China Sea.

2. 4-Day Itinerary: City Exploration and Cultural Immersion

Day 1: City Highlights

- Morning: - Explore Marina Bay Sands and take in sweeping views of the city from the SkyPark Observation Deck.
- Visit the ArtScience Museum and discover its interactive exhibits.
- Afternoon: - Have lunch at Lau Pa Sat, a famous hawker centre in the heart of the city. - Visit the National Gallery Singapore and enjoy its collection of Southeast Asian art.
- Evening: - Take a walk along Marina Bay and watch the Spectra light and water show.

Day 2: Cultural Immersion

- Morning: - Visit the Singapore Botanic Gardens and enjoy its lush greenery and beautiful orchid garden. - Have breakfast at a nearby cafe.

- Afternoon: - Explore Little India and visit the Sri Veeramakaliamman Temple and Mustafa Centre. - Have lunch at an Indian restaurant and taste authentic Indian cuisine.

- Evening: - Take a walking tour of Kampong Glam and visit the Sultan Mosque and Arab Street. - Have dinner at a Middle Eastern place and try dishes like shawarma and falafel.

Day 3: Neighbourhood Exploration

- Morning: - Explore the historic area of Tiong Bahru and visit its trendy cafes and boutique shops. - Have breakfast at a neighbourhood cafe and try traditional Singaporean kaya toast and kopi.

- Afternoon: - Visit the Singapore Zoo and enjoy a guided tram ride through the zoo's different zones. - Have lunch at the zoo's Ah Meng Restaurant.

- Evening: - Explore the nightlife of Clarke Quay and enjoy dinner at one of the many riverside restaurants.

Day 4: Day Trip to Pulau Ubin

- Morning: - Take a boat to Pulau Ubin, a rustic island off the coast of Singapore. - Rent a bike and discover the island's lush forests, mangroves, and traditional villages.

- Afternoon: - Have lunch at one of the island's seafood restaurants. - Visit Chek Jawa Wetlands and enjoy its mangrove boardwalks and coastal trails.
- Evening: - Take the boat back to Singapore and relax at your hotel.

No matter how long you plan to stay in Singapore, these sample schedules will help you make the most of your time in the Lion City. Whether you're interested in discovering the city's iconic landmarks, immersing yourself in its rich culture, or venturing off the beaten path, Singapore has something for everyone. So pack your bags, discover the city with confidence, and make unforgettable memories in one of Asia's most dynamic and exciting destinations!

Walking Tours and Self Guided Tours

One of the best ways to discover Singapore and fully immerse yourself in its vibrant culture and rich heritage is by embarking on walking tours and self-guided tours. Whether you're a history buff, a foodie, or an outdoor lover, there's a tour for everyone. Here's why you should consider visiting Singapore on foot:

1. Freedom to Explore at Your Own Pace:
- Walking tours and self-guided tours allow you to explore Singapore at your own pace, without feeling rushed or limited by a strict schedule.
- Take your time to enjoy the city's iconic landmarks, hidden gems, and charming neighbourhoods at your leisure.

2. Flexibility and Customization:
- With self-guided tours, you have the flexibility to create your schedule based on your interests and preferences.
- Choose the attractions you want to visit, the neighbourhoods you want to explore, and the length of your tour to create a personalised experience.

3. Cost-effective Travel choice:
- Walking tours and self-guided tours are often more budget-friendly than guided tours, making them an excellent choice for budget-conscious travellers.

- Save money on tour fees and transportation costs while still having an immersive travel experience.

4. Discover Hidden Gems and Local Favourites:

- Walking tours and self-guided tours allow you to discover hidden gems and local favourites that may not be included in standard guided tours.

- Explore charming neighbourhoods, bustling markets, and off-the-beaten-path sites that only locals know about.

5. Cultural Immersion and Local Interaction:

- By exploring Singapore on foot, you'll have more opportunities to interact with locals, immerse yourself in the city's culture, and gain a better understanding of its rich history.

- Visit local markets, street food stalls, and traditional shops to experience Singapore like a local.

6. Stay Active and Healthy:

- Walking tours are a great way to stay active and healthy while travelling. - Explore Singapore's beautiful parks, gardens, and seaside promenades while getting some exercise and fresh air.

7. Safety and Security:

- Singapore is one of the safest cities in the world, making it an ideal location for walking tours and self-guided tours.

- Enjoy peace of mind as you explore the city's streets, parks, and sites without worrying about safety concerns.

Popular Walking Tours and Self-guided Tours in Singapore:

1. tradition Trails:

- Explore Singapore's rich history and tradition with a self-guided heritage trail.

- Visit historic landmarks, cultural sites, and museums to learn about the city's diverse cultural history.

2. Food Tours:

- Embark on a self-guided food tour and try Singapore's diverse culinary delights.

- Visit hawker shops, street food stalls, and local eateries to taste traditional Singaporean dishes like laksa, chicken rice, and chilli crab.

3. Nature Walks:

- Discover Singapore's lush green areas and natural beauty with a self-guided nature walk.

- Explore parks, gardens, and nature areas like the Singapore Botanic Gardens, MacRitchie Reservoir Park, and Pulau Ubin.

4. Cultural Neighborhood Tours:

- Explore Singapore's vibrant areas with a self-guided cultural tour.

- Visit Chinatown, Little India, Kampong Glam, and other cultural enclaves to experience the city's diverse cultural history.

5. Street Art Tours:

- Discover Singapore's lively street art scene with a self-guided street art tour. - Explore areas like Tiong Bahru, Haji Lane, and Joo Chiat to admire colourful murals, graffiti, and street art installations.

Walking tours and self-guided tours offer a flexible, cost-effective, and immersive way to discover Singapore's rich culture, history, and heritage. Whether you're interested in history, food, nature, or art, there's a tour for every visitor. So lace up your walking shoes, grab a map, and start on an unforgettable journey through the vibrant streets of Singapore!

7 DAY ITINERARY

Day 1: Explore the City's Iconic Landmarks

- Morning: Start your day with a walk to Marina Bay Sands. Take in sweeping views of the city from the SkyPark Observation Deck.

- Afternoon: Visit the ArtScience Museum and enjoy its interactive exhibits.

- Evening: Take a leisurely walk along Marina Bay and watch the Spectra light and water show.

Day 2: Dive into Singapore's Culture and Heritage

- Morning: Explore Chinatown. Visit the Buddha Tooth Relic Temple and Museum and explore the bustling streets full with shops and street food stalls.

- Afternoon: Discover the vibrant area of Little India. Visit the Sri Veeramakaliamman Temple, explore Mustafa Centre, and indulge in delicious Indian food.

- Evening: Take a walking tour of Kampong Glam. Visit the Sultan Mosque and Arab Street, and enjoy dinner at a Middle Eastern restaurant.

Day 3: Nature and Wildlife

- Morning: Explore the Singapore Botanic Gardens. Visit the National Orchid Garden and enjoy a leisurely walk through the lush greenery.

- Afternoon: Visit the Singapore Zoo. Enjoy a guided tram ride through the zoo's different zones and get up close to over 2,800 animals.

- Evening: Experience the Night Safari. Embark on a nocturnal journey and see the zoo come alive after dark.

Day 4: Day Trip to Sentosa Island

- Morning: Take a cable car ride to Sentosa Island. Visit Universal Studios Singapore and enjoy thrilling rides and activities.

- Afternoon: Have lunch at one of the many places on Sentosa Island. Visit S.E.A. Aquarium and wonder at over 100,000 marine animals.

- Evening: Relax on the beach or take a relaxing walk along the Sentosa Boardwalk.

Day 5: Food and Shopping

- Morning: Explore Tiong Bahru. Visit trendy cafes and boutique shops and enjoy breakfast at a local cafe.

- Afternoon: Visit Orchard Road for a shopping trip.

Explore the many shopping malls and shops and indulge in some retail therapy.

- Evening: Explore the lively nightlife of Clarke Quay. Enjoy dinner at one of the many riverside restaurants and bars.

Day 6: Cultural Neighbourhoods

- Morning: Visit Kampong Glam. Explore the Sultan Mosque, Arab Street, and Haji Lane.

- Afternoon: Explore the historic neighbourhood of Joo Chiat. Visit the colourful Peranakan shophouses and indulge in delicious Peranakan food.

- Evening: Experience the lively nightlife of Bugis Street. Explore the busy night market and enjoy street food and shopping.

Day 7: Explore Singapore's Parks and Gardens

- Morning: Visit Gardens by the Bay. Explore the Flower Dome, Cloud Forest, and Supertree Grove.

- Afternoon: Visit the Singapore Flyer. Enjoy panoramic views of the city from one of the world's biggest observation wheels.

- Evening: Take a water cruise along the Singapore water. Admire the city's iconic sites illuminated at night.

Experience the best of Singapore with this thorough 7-day itinerary. From iconic sites and cultural neighbourhoods to delicious cuisine and vibrant nightlife, Singapore has something for everyone. Enjoy your trip to the Lion City!

CONCLUSION

Congratulations! You've hit the end of our comprehensive Singapore travel guide for 2024, your ultimate companion to exploring the Lion City in style. Singapore is a dynamic destination that offers a perfect blend of rich history, vibrant culture, delicious food, and breathtaking attractions.

From iconic sites like Marina Bay Sands and Gardens by the Bay to cultural enclaves like Chinatown, Little India, and Kampong Glam, Singapore has something for everyone. Whether you're a foodie looking to indulge in mouth watering street food, a history buff eager to explore the city's heritage, or an adventure seeker ready to take on exciting day trips and excursions, Singapore will captivate you with its charm and diversity.

Our travel guide has provided you with all the information you need to plan an unforgettable trip to Singapore, including tips on the best time to visit, visa requirements, transportation choices, accommodation, dining, shopping, nightlife, and more.

Explore the city's iconic sites, immerse yourself in its vibrant culture, indulge in delicious cuisine, and create memories that will last a lifetime. Whether you're going solo, with family, or with friends, Singapore promises an unforgettable experience that will leave you longing to return.

So pack your bags, lace up your walking shoes, and get ready to start on the adventure of a lifetime in the Lion City. Singapore awaits, ready to enchant you with its beauty, charm, and boundless possibilities. Start planning your dream trip to Singapore today, and get ready to experience the magic of this incredible destination directly.

Your adventure starts here. Welcome to Singapore, where every moment is a new find and every experience is an unforgettable memory. Let the journey begin!

Made in the USA
Columbia, SC
27 November 2024